27.7.25

The
UNNATURAL
Habitat
of a
Cat Lady

DANI ELIAS

Editor: Sofia Artola Diaz
Proofreader: Katie Rosenthal

Contents

Content Warning

The book is a contemporary Romcom which includes scenes of a sexual nature and adult content.

The book may also contain some or all of these:

- BDSM

- Depression

If any of this serves as a trigger for you, please decide if this is the book for you.

Finally, the book is set in England and British English spelling is used throughout. That means a lot of times you'll find an "S" where you may expect a "Z". And our ass has an extra Rrrr to it ;-).

Dedication

To all those who want to be a *Good Girl* for a good guy

Special thanks to my author friend Eliza's husband's testicles for providing inspiration for one of my favourite scenes in this book.

Set the mood...

Want a soundtrack to the book?

Check out the Chapter titles or scan/click here:

You can also find a copy of the full playlist at the back of

the book!

Couldn't have done it without...

The story of *The Unnatural Habitat of a Cat Lady* has been "living" in my brain for over a year. I have changed little bits of the story here and there, dropped some characters and added others but the essence of what makes Ben and Amelia who they are never changed. Neither did my desire to make sure that any references to the BDSM community are accurate and realistic.

I did a lot of reading and researching but nothing is as valuable as getting your information straight from the "horse's mouth", so to speak.

Therefore, I would like to say a big thank you to the Kinky Events Community (www.kinkyevents.co.uk)! They allowed me into their circle, patiently answered all my questions and gave me a great understanding of what's important.

A special thank you has to go to Ryan who volunteered to alpha read the book to make sure that Ben fits the profile of a pleasure dom. He provided some super helpful insights and tips. I don't think I have ever had a saucier conversation with a complete stranger before but I did it all for you, my lovely readers. I can also proudly say that the book is pleasure dom approved because Ryan confirmed that "Ben is really good as he is." (I'm pretty sure that was his way of telling me "Good Girl")

To all you amazing people at the Kinky Events Community
munity
and especially Ryan
THANK YOU!

The UNNATURAL Habitat of a Cat Lady

1

Fuck You

Amelia

I CAN FEEL HIS eyes on me. *Don't say it. Don't you bloody say it.*

"Maybe we need to get an expert in to advise us on the security situation." *That little twerp said it.* I glare at Richard across the table. He just won't accept that I, as the Head of Security Risk Management, am in charge of security (it's in the title!) when it comes to trips our staff take.

"I mean, what do *we* really know about the risks in—"

"It's my job to know," I cut Richard off. When he throws in the "we," he really means me. Back when I was hired he was baffled by the idea that a woman could possibly be in charge of security, and instead was heavily rooting for an ex-army guy who also applied for the job.

"With all due respect—," Richard starts. *Give me a fucking break.* The minute someone mutters with all due respect, you know they mean the exact opposite.

"Richard, Amelia's right. It's her job to assess the situation and I'm not having this conversation yet again. If she says we need risk committee approval, then we do. So put a business plan together and explain why it is essential for one of your team to be present on the ground rather than liaising from London." *Uh, what is this, did he just side with me, like, for the first time ever?* Graham is making it crystal clear that he won't accept any objections. So far, Graham has agreed every time Richard has pushed for an "expert", and I have had to reach out to yet another security consultant to come in look at my assessment and mitigation plan and then, in a condescending tone, explain to me how they would do it, which usually is exactly the same way I had proposed, just in different words. It's a waste of resources and time, let alone a constant source of frustration to me.

I was hired a year ago when Lisa, the owner of Connect Beyond Borders, secured major investment to take the company global. We provide communications solutions to the NGO sector, more specific to aid agencies working in remote areas. When the company started, Lisa and her partner Shaker offered advice as consultants, but with the new investment the company has hired engineers and technicians to provide innovative solutions connecting aid workers with their offices.

I'm aware that I sound like our company brochure but that's because I've attended about fifteen million corporate events where this line was repeated so often that it sounded as if our sales team were peddling a new religion.

"If there's nothing else, just a reminder that I need your budget review by the end of next week." Graham dismisses us. "Oh, and Amelia, can you stay for a minute?" I watch as the others file out of the COO's office. He is one of the few with his own office in the otherwise open plan concept. , His office is surrounded by glass on three sides, so we call it the fish tank behind his back.

Samira, the Director of HR gives me a quick side eye as if to say "What the fuck does he want from you?" before scuttling from the office. She is probably the only one at work that I am close to and I know she'll be waiting at her desk for me to give her the gossip once I come back.

The glass door falls shut behind the last person leaving the office.

"Right. I had a look at your budget and you're way over and we still have two months left in the financial year."

Graham looks at me expectantly, as if I could explain it all away as a fluke.

"Forty percent of my budget has been used up by the security consultants you wanted me to hire for the Syria and Yemen trips."

"And you never said that would exceed your budget," he replies. I am waiting for him to tell me that this is all a joke. Nothing.

"But you know how much these consultants charge."

"It's not my job to manage your budget." *What a dick.* I try to calm my breathing because I can feel anger rising. "Amelia, you are a senior member of staff, and if you don't agree with a decision in your department, for whatever reason, I expect you to fight it and not let Richard bully you into it."

"But you agreed with him."

"Because you didn't object."

"I did."

"Well, not very strongly. In any case your expenditure is too high. Lisa has agreed to top it up a little but if you need any additional funding for any experts for the rest of the year you'll need to make an application directly to her." *Aha!* So, this is why he sided with me in the meeting. Lisa had words with him and he threw me under the bus. There

is a lump in my throat that makes it difficult to swallow, a
ball of anger that I try desperately to suppress.

"Fine." I grab my pad. "Anything else?" In my head I
sound super pissed off but I know that Graham won't
notice a difference. I am a master at concealing what I really
feel.

"Can you have a look at your budget and let me know if
there are any activities you need to postpone?"

"Sure." I leave the meeting room without another word.
That will show him. I glance back and see him typing away
on his laptop. I'm not sure he's even noticed that I have
left.

*I hate this job, I hate this job, I haaaaate this job. Richard
is such a wanker! And Graham, throwing me under the bus
like that. Argh. I swear they're both a couple of donkeys with
their heads up their arses. I hope they get a nasty case of
genital warts and have to explain it to their partners. Ugh,
why am I surrounded by utter tossers? Grit your teeth and
smile, Amelia. Just another day in paradise.*

"What happened?" Samira asks as I take a seat next to her
on the bank of desks in the far corner. These are the most
popular seats in our open plan office. You have to be quick
to get them booked before everyone else has a chance, but
Samira and I both have reminders in our calendars and if

one forgets the other one will book the desk for both of us.

"I overspent on my budget and apparently it's my fault because I didn't object strongly enough when Richard and Graham railroaded me on the Syria and Yemen trips."

"Dicks!"

"Samira!" I admonish but give her an appreciative smile. "I'm sure as Director of HR you should not say that."

"Maybe. But as your friend and as a woman with a brain I call it as it is." She shrugs and returns her attention to her spreadsheet.

"Want to go for a coffee after work?" she asks whilst formatting a table. Samira and I first bonded over our love for Excel. If you find someone else who gets a metaphorical boner for conditional formatting, you have to become friends, right?

"I can't. I'm meeting the girls for dinner," I shoot her a sad look. Honestly, I'd rather have a cuppa with Samira, but it's been ages since I caught up with my friends. Usually when we do manage to meet, for them it's all about hitting the booze and taking the mickey out of me. I'm not much of a drinker, though——it tends to bring me down, and Smutty, my feline overlord, can't stand the smell of alcohol on me. Yeah, my cat rules me with an iron paw, but those big yellow eyes in his squishy black face? They're impossible to resist. So I'm a good subservient and stick to lemonade. There's nothing duller than being the lone teetotaller in the room. What drunk people find amusing is about as entertaining to sober me as a trip to the gynaecologist.

"Uh, the witches of Battersea," Samira rolls her eyes. She met Miranda and Bea once and took an instant dislike to them. She doesn't get why I let them insult me. I tried to explain that it's just a bit of banter but she thinks they're bullies. They are my oldest friends though. We grew up together in a small village not far from London and have known each other for donkey's years. Whilst I still live in the village——I love that place——, they convinced their other halves to move to a fancy estate in trendy Battersea where they are stay-at-home mums.

Bea is married with two kids and Miranda's wedding is happening in a few weeks. Sim-Sim (or Simon Gordon junior for those not in the know) is finally taking her down the aisle after they had a child out of wedlock, and it's all everyone can talk about. Both their families were in uproar when Miranda and Simon announced that they were pregnant before getting hitched, like we were still in the 1950s. The christening of Simon junior junior was tense, to say the least.

But however different our lives may be, they are my oldest friends and really they are some of the few people I have in my life. I was never particularly close with my parents and now that they live in Madeira——Mum needs the warmer climate——, I see them once a year at the most. There are a few people I occasionally meet up with, but I wouldn't consider them friends. They are more acquaintances. Getting close to people isn't my strong suit. So, there's Samira at work, and then there're Bea and Miranda.

"You should join us sometime," I suggest and Samira raises an eyebrow. "Honestly, they are nice." I mean, Miranda is definitely the nicer of the two. Bea can be testing sometimes.

Before Samira can reply her mobile rings, interrupting our conversation. I open my emails; the first one is from Richard with the subject line "Consultants we could use." *I hate this job.*

T HE SCREEN OF MY phone lights up when I tap it. Ten past six. They're half an hour late again. They're always late. Always. And I don't get it. They're mums with nannies. Surely you can plan to leave the house on time to be at the restaurant when we agreed.

"Sorry, sorry, sorry," Miranda squeaks dramatically as she takes a seat. "Simon needed some help with his homework and then Sim-Sim called and asked me to drop off some documents he'd forgotten at home. Just be glad you're single," she exhales to show how exhausting her life is.

"That's okay,—" I don't get to finish my sentence as Bea drops into the remaining chair. Both immediately start complaining about their lives and try to outdo each other with who is the busiest and whose kids are the most gifted. As always, I fade into the background. The most I could share is that Smutty managed to vomit his furball in my slipper last night.

"So, how are you?" Bea addresses me.

"I'm… fine." I never know what else to say. My life revolves around work, Smutty and my adventure trips abroad. "Well, aside from my boss throwing me under the bus." I laugh a little apprehensively. I have tried talking to them about work before, but they didn't show much interest.

"Ah, men are just idiots. Look at my husband to be. Sim-Sim told me to get the purple flowers because they're his mother's favourite because *what does it really matter*, and... I'm sorry, Amelia. We were talking about you. It's just this wedding's driving me crazy. So, any interesting dates on the horizon?" she asks with a sheepish look on her face.

Oh, here comes the dreaded conversation. I know exactly how this will go. I'll confirm that I am indeed still just dating my vibrator, aka I mumble "No, nobody." And that causes them both to give me a sorrowful head tilt and a sad, "Maybe you're too picky." We have been down this road a million times.

"I thought you just said men are idiots?" I counter Miranda's question. I'm really not in the mood for the usual pity party.

"You just need to train your significant other properly," Bea laughs and takes a sip of my lemonade. "Eww, I forgot you don't drink."

"You mean you trained your husband like a poodle?" I can't help myself, I had to say it. Two pairs of eyes bore into me.

"You can't expect to find the perfect guy, Amelia. You have to make him perfect," Bea rebukes, giving me a stern look. It stings a bit because she's suggesting that, naturally, the issue lies with me. But it also makes me squirm a tad because I don't want to have to "train" a guy. I'm not searching for Mr. Flawless; I'm yearning for someone whose quirks fit mine like a jigsaw puzzle. I'm more into the "let's embrace each other's weirdness" vibe.

But then, I'm the only single person at the table. Maybe Bea and Miranda are right and I'm just a bit green, but I've been with guys who seemed like they needed "fixing," and you can't fix a person. Everyone has their own personality, and I believe you should love them for it, not despite it.

"Well, maybe you'll find out soon," Bea announces excitedly before grabbing her menu, like she doesn't already know she'll have the salad. She's on a strict fitness regime and I can't remember ever having gone for a meal with her when she didn't eat a salad. There is always a twang of guilt when I stuff my face with a creamy lasagne or juicy steak whilst she scrapes dressing off her lettuce to reduce the calorie intake, but then the food touches my tongue and the flavours explode and I tell myself fuck it. This is worth the squishy bits on my hips, and arse... and, well, thighs.

"What do you mean?" Miranda probes, but before Bea can reply the waiter interrupts to take our orders. One salad and one plain chicken breast with broccoli for the girls, mac and cheese for me. *Fuck it!* I have a feeling that when Bea tells me what she's done I'll probably need some comfort food.

Bea leans back and looks at us with a smirk. She pauses dramatically before holding up her phone and announcing, "I've signed you up for online dating."

2

Play With Fire

Amelia

I CAN FEEL RAGE rising in me, but I try to keep my breathing steady.

"Excuse me?" My voice sounds a little bit shaky, but the others don't seem to notice.

"You need a date for Miranda's wedding," she shrugs and opens an app.

"Oh, exciting! Show us!" Miranda giggles and the two focus on Bea's phone. I'm frozen in anger. That's what I do. Inside, there's a war raging, but on the outside, I present myself as calm, collected, and completely unaffected. It can be handy in certain life situations, but right now,

I'd rather unleash a full-on banshee scream than sit there, seemingly unfazed by it all.

"No, she can't get that one," Bea says and swipes left. "Out of her league, out of her league, out of her league." Her fingers fly over the screen and keep swiping left. I squint and look closer. Guy after guy in dark suits with broody looks. *What app is this?* Then I spot something that makes me gasp.

"Excuse me, why does it say 'Daddy Dom' on that guy's profile?" On the screen is a silver fox called Sam. He's wearing a white shirt with his sleeves rolled up and holding a belt in his hands. The smirk on his face makes it perfectly clear what he's after.

"It's a BDSM app," Bea replies, shooting me a questioning look. "You are into that, right?"

"What?" I splutter.

"BDSM," she says slowly just as the waiter puts a drink on the table. He snorts and I want to die. Right here, I want to die.

"What makes you think that?" I whisper shout.

"Well, you read the books."

"I read ONE book." Ages ago they saw a dark romance on my Kindle and ever since they've been joking that I'm into BDSM. I mean, I do read some very smutty stuff (and the girls don't need to know that this is a regular occurrence.) But there are a lot of elements to BDSM that are really not my thing.

"See," Bea smirks, like one book is enough to make me a subscriber to Dominatrix Weekly. Miranda giggles, but stops when I don't join in. I snatch the phone from the table.

"Hey," Bea objects and tries to grab it back but I'm too quick.

"Where did you get the photo from?" I inhale sharply when I see the profile picture. It's me in bed with Smutty curled up in front of me.

"I took a screenshot when we had our Sunday morning video call a few weeks ago," she shrugs like it's not a big deal.

I gasp for air and try to formulate words but nothing comes to mind. Instead, I get up and walk away from them. I find a quiet corner and take a deep breath. My fingers fly over the screen until I find the profile settings. There's a moment where I contemplate deleting the account, but instead I change the password and email address linked to it, replacing them with my own. Essentially, I'm shutting Bea out. The only justification I can offer is curiosity; that's why I'm not deleting the account.

"Here." I hold out her phone as I get back to the table and she gives me a miffed look.

"What did you do?"

"Removed the account." *From your phone.* "Don't do that again!" My voice is cold.

Miranda looks uncomfortable from me to Bea and then puts some veggies in her mouth as if she doesn't want to be dragged into this argument.

"Do you want to die as an old cat lady?" Bea asks through a mouthful of her rabbit food. If her husband could see her now. He's like thirty-fifth in line to the throne or something, and she acts all snobbish around him. Totally different from how she is with us. I guess he "trained" her.

"I didn't ask for help. And why is it so important to you that I'm in a relationship?"

"It's not normal to be single at our age," Bea scoffs. "And the pool is getting smaller and smaller." I don't need to ask what she means by that.

"Says who?" I ask defiantly, crossing my arms in front of my chest.

"I mean, you probably don't want children this old," Miranda suggests, trying to argue my side even if her comment feels like another dig. I'm forty-one. Fair enough, it would be harder now but it wouldn't require a medical miracle.

"But you don't want to die alone either," Bea adds. And here we are with death again. I'm forty-freak'n-one. I could live another forty years. Again that would not constitute a medical miracle.

"I have plenty of time to find someone. But you know what, even if I don't, I won't die alone. I'll have Smutty. Although he may chew up my face if nobody finds me early enough," I give them a smirk and take a big spoonful of pasta.

Bea's eyes fall on my food and she is about to give me a snide comment about it, I'm sure, but I cut her off.

"So, what are you going to do about the flowers?" I divert the attention from me to Miranda. Just like every other time, this works like a treat. Both like nothing better than to talk about weddings. Shoes, flowers, music, who will bitch about the food, who can't sit next to whom because they hate each other. I don't get it. I'm a bit of a wedding-phobe. I like the idea of being married, of promising one special person that you'll be there for them for the rest of your life. But the idea of a wedding with uncomfortable clothes, overpriced meals and forced dancing makes me shudder. Lucky for me, Miranda's soon-to-be husband only has one groomsman so she can only have one bridesmaid. I have never volunteered quicker for anything than sitting out bridesmaid duties.

I T'S AFTER TEN BY the time I get back to my small cottage on the outskirts of Little Hadlow. I've lived in this village all my life. The house I grew up in is only two streets over from my cottage. Little Hadlow is a stone's throw from Sevenoaks and close enough to London for a daily commute to work. So, if I ever fancy a bit of city life, it's there for the taking. Yet, despite its proximity to the capital, Little Hadlow still feels like a whole different world. Rural, quiet, less pretentious and more ... homely. Even after my parents moved, I never really wanted to live anywhere else .

As I approach the front door all seems quiet but I'm sure I'm being watched. I can almost feel his eyes bore into me from the darkness behind the ground floor window. Smutty won't let me hear the end of returning home so late and making him wait for his dinner. He's a little drama queen... drama king, just a bit of a pain in the arse to be honest. I found him when he was tiny, drenched from the rain and shaking from the cold. I searched for his mum and owner but couldn't find anyone and so I took him home, pepped him up and ever since my house has been his kingdom. What he wants, he gets.

I push the door open carefully and I'm immediately greeted by a pitiful cry. He can't be that hungry as I always leave him enough food, but he won't stop this caterwauling until he can be sure I have learned my lesson.

Huh, maybe I am a submissive? I'm a submissive to my cat. The thought causes me to chuckle, much to Smutty's displeasure. He ups his wailing a nudge and rubs against my legs. I almost stumble over him in the dark.

"Smutty, cut it out!" I feel my way along the wall until my fingers find the light switch. In the dim shine of the single lamp swinging from the ceiling I can see that Smutty has rummaged through my laundry again. Two pairs of knickers are strewn around the living room floor.

"Oh, come on, did you need to do this?" I point at my underwear. He just bumps his head into my leg. All he's interested in is being fed. When I have to travel to work I leave him dry food but what he really wants is some stinking wet cat food. I hate the smell but, well, he's the boss.

Smutty is at the limit of his patience whilst I hang up my coat and fiddle for my phone in my coat pocket. He starts to nibble on my Achilles tendon. With my shoes off he has full access and he doesn't hesitate.

"Stop it," I laugh and jump out of the way. "Fine, come on then." I walk towards the kitchen and Smutty overtakes me, making little chirping noises. *That's my happy boy.* I drop my phone on the tiny kitchen table and grab a tin of food. The race is on: if I'm not quick, he'll sink his teeth into the back of my foot again.

The plate with his food hasn't even touched the floor when Smutty wolfs down the first bite. You'd think he hadn't eaten in days. I pick up my phone and leave him to it. I head to my bedroom, switching off all lights on the way there.

I love my cottage. It's quaint, it's cosy, and I feel at home here. Aside from the living room and kitchen on the ground floor, there's a small downstairs bathroom in a nook under the stairs. On the first floor I have my bedroom, a small office which doubles as a guest bedroom, and a bathroom with a giant bath. The tub is my pride and joy. It's not only large, but also extra deep with part of it lowered into the floor. This means that when I'm having a bath I am actually fully submerged. not like in normal sized bathtubs where you have to decide between sticking your legs out so your boobs are covered or freezing your nipples off so that your legs are covered.

Speaking about a bath. Right now that sounds like a great idea; I could do with some relaxing. My mind is still reeling from the fact that Bea has signed me up for a dating app. A BDSM dating app. I eye my phone on my bed as I take off my cardigan. I'm angry, yes, but I'm also curious. I mean, it's not that I haven't fantasised about being pushed up against a wall whilst getting pounded hard by a broody Alpha. Not sure that qualifies as BDSM though. It does in my world of vanilla sex.

Eventually curiosity wins and I jump onto my bed. I should finish changing but instead I sit there in just my bra and trousers as my finger slides over the glass to unlock it. When the home screen flashes up I download the app. As soon as I'm logged in I see a tiny number three next to the message icon. I hesitate for a moment before I tap on it.

Christopher

Hello, Amelia. Are you going to be a good girl for me?

Yup, no. No, no. I click delete and the next message pops up.

Thomas

I'd like to see your pussy.

Sure, let me take a quick picture. I shake my head. *People!* I should really check what details Bea has put up on my profile.

Ben

Hi Amelia!

That's it? I wait a little longer, but he doesn't send anything else. I click on his profile. It's another guy in a shirt with rolled up sleeves. Only the bottom half of his face is visible. *Pleasure dom.* That's the category he's chosen for himself. I'm not sure what that means.

I open the search engine on my phone, choose anonymous browsing and type in the words pleasure dom.

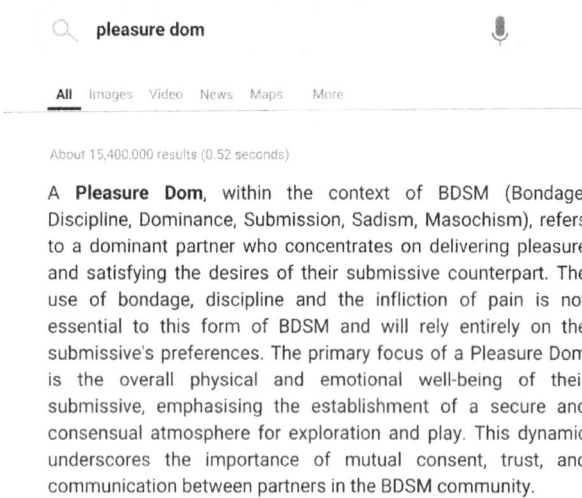

Q.   **pleasure dom**   🎤

All Images Video News Maps   More

About 15,400,000 results (0.52 seconds)

A **Pleasure Dom**, within the context of BDSM (Bondage, Discipline, Dominance, Submission, Sadism, Masochism), refers to a dominant partner who concentrates on delivering pleasure and satisfying the desires of their submissive counterpart. The use of bondage, discipline and the infliction of pain is not essential to this form of BDSM and will rely entirely on the submissive's preferences. The primary focus of a Pleasure Dom is the overall physical and emotional well-being of their submissive, emphasising the establishment of a secure and consensual atmosphere for exploration and play. This dynamic underscores the importance of mutual consent, trust, and communication between partners in the BDSM community.

There is a nervous twitch in my tummy and a tingling between my legs. That actually doesn't sound scary. That sounds... exciting. I tap the message and reply:

Me

Hi Ben!

Shit! I turn the screen off and throw my phone on my bed. I can't believe I did that. I just got in touch with a pleasure dom!

3

If I Could Turn Back Time

Ben

I CAN FEEL A hammering behind my eyes. The only light in the room is the glimmer coming from my laptop and the small desk lamp. I should've switched on the main light before this video conference started. Two hours in, I regret my laziness. Just as much as I regret attending this thing in the first place. There isn't much in it for our company joining this conference for young entrepreneurs, but Nebula Tech Ventures is a top tech firm in Silicon Valley, and we're trying to agree a partnership with them.

So, when they invited us to their event it was difficult to say no.

Aside from the voice of the presenter coming from my laptop the office is eerily quiet. Even the cleaner has called it a day. I hit the button on my mobile and see that it's past ten. When Coop and I kicked off our company over a decade ago, we pulled insane hours. There were times when we'd sleep at the office because going home seemed pointless. Now, our main company oversees six others, and we've scaled our hours back a bit. Still, I often find myself working until late at night. Coop is finally in the relationship he had been dreaming of for so long and rarely stays beyond six these days. Honestly, I could probably leave sooner if I wanted, but I've got nothing and nobody waiting for me. An empty house, an empty office——what's the difference?

I love my work and I'm not a monk. I have the occasional date and there is Gina, my... acquaintance with benefits for a lack of a better word. But I'm forty-two and I'm starting to wonder if I'm not wasting my years with just work and casual dating. If there isn't more to life.

Gina and I actually tried to date properly when we both lived in New York. She runs her own skin care company and spends half her time in the US and half her time back here. We bonded over our love for England and our sexual preferences, but quickly realised that we just don't have the right feelings for each other. She's beautiful and fun and a good submissive, but she doesn't make my heart race and she doesn't make me think of a future together. Not that this would even be an option at the moment. I haven't seen her in a while because she has been dating a new dom and it seemed serious between them, and I respect that. Neither of us believes in cheating.

My eyes slide back to the clock. Fifteen more minutes and then this part of the workshop will be over and I can sign off. My stomach protests loudly because the last thing I had to eat was the sandwich Gladys brought me at noon. Gladys is our office angel and has been with Coop and me since we started the company. Last week was her sixtieth birthday and that made me realise that she's not far from retiring. She deserves nothing more than to put her feet up, but the thought of running the company without her there does not fill me with joy.

My fingers fiddle with the phone again and, on autopilot, I open up my favourite dating app. I've dabbled in the BDSM scene since my late twenties, but in the last five years I found what really works for me. I don't get my kink from pain or bondage; I get it from providing endless pleasure to my submissives. And the easiest way to meet like-minded people is this specialist app.

I have a few messages waiting for me but I disregard them. Some people don't bother to read the person's profile and that's how I end up with messages from women looking for daddy doms, which I don't do, and dominatrixes who want to peg me, which I'm definitely not into.

As there are no interesting prospects in my inbox I start swiping. Left, left, right, left. I don't worry too much about the photos. After all, I'm only showing the bottom half of my face myself, so who am I to judge?

Left, right, right... the next photo makes me pause. It's of a blonde woman lying on a bed. She's in the background with a black cat dominating the front of the picture. With her fair locks and white nighty, she looks as innocent as they come even if her age reads forty-one.

Something looks familiar. Very familiar. I cast my eye over the details on her profile. Amelia. I sit up straight. *Fucking hell.* I zoom into the picture. And there they are. The blue-grey eyes I haven't seen in twenty years even if I thought about them often. *Amelia. My Amelia.* My heart starts racing as memories flood my brain. Some amazing ones, some incredible sexy ones, and some heart-wrenching painful ones. And it's those painful thoughts that should stop me from reaching out to her.

Huh, who am I kidding? No way can I miss this opportunity. There is a reason why I settled back into the village we grew up in after moving back from the States. Be it when heading to the shops or on my Sunday morning run, the hope of bumping into her is always there. I know she still lives in Little Hadlow but I haven't dared to ask our mutual friends where her place is exactly. It's not that I hope to win her back. I think the chances of that are nil. All I want is an opportunity to say sorry and explain myself. That's it.

"Ben, are there any closing words you have for our young hopefuls?" I had completely forgotten that I'm on a video call.

"Sure," I start summarising the pros and cons of being an entrepreneur as my eyes drift down to my phone, making sure I'm hitting the right keys as I type *Hi Amelia* in the app. Not particularly creative, but I just want to make sure I don't lose her profile when I close my phone to focus on the rest of the video call. *No, I can't lose her.* Surely it must be fate to find her on this app. What is she doing on a BDSM app? I mean, sex with Amelia was... amazing, but I don't think she was particularly adventurous. I would be lying if I said I wasn't intrigued, but what I really want to know is if she still hates me. *Yes, that's the only reason I'm reaching out. The only reason.*

Now, how am I going to play this? I can't really come out and say, "Surprise, it's me!" She'll block me immediately. No, I need to at least get her to meet up with me. I finally want a chance to explain myself. And to say sorry.

"Can we all give Ben a big round of virtual applause?" the host of the workshop, whose name I have completely forgotten, asks the attendees. Everyone who is showing on my screen raises their hands and gives me some weird finger wiggling gesture. I bite my lip to avoid showing how ridiculous I find it.

"Thank you for having me and good luck to you all." I sign off and shoot a message to Omar, my driver. Having a company driver is one of the few luxuries Coop and I allow ourselves. I drive my own car on the weekends. But Coop and I both hate public transport, and finding anywhere to park when heading to meetings is usually a nightmare. So it made sense for us to have company drivers. We've got two actually; one handling the morning shift and the other tackling the evening slot. Roger, who picks me up in the morning, has a busier schedule during the day with staff coming and going from meetings. In contrast, Omar works from three until whenever I finish, leaving him with little to do after five once most staff have left for the day. But he's cool with it, always assuring me that he puts the downtime to good use by hitting the books. It never fails to amuse me when he talks about his studies; after all, he's in his late thirties, not much younger than me. Omar spent

his twenties globetrotting and then another decade settling down and reintegrating to society. It was then that he
decided he wanted to work on his career and get a degree.
I admire him really. I'm not sure if I'd have the energy to
start all over again.

With my phone in one hand and my jacket in the other
I step into the lift and lean against the back wall. I loosen
my tie and immediately feel more relaxed. Ties are not my
cup of tea. If I could, I'd roll into the office in jeans, but I
need to wear suits for meetings, and there aren't any days
when I don't have meetings lined up.

The dreaded suit also causes me issues when dating
sometimes. Thanks to certain films and books, everyone
anticipates a dom in a suit. On more than one occasion
a woman, new to the scene has turned into a proper brat
when I've turned up for our date in jeans and a T-shirt,
not believing that I'm a dom, just because I wasn't wearing
what they were expecting.

That thought brings me back to the app. *Amelia*. I'm
itching to see if she's replied. *Wait until you're in the car.*
I'm not sure if I'm edging myself here or if I'm just too
scared to find out she's ignored my message, or even worse,
blocked me. I have knots in my stomach again. I can't
remember the last time I was so nervous.

"Hey, Omar," I call out as I settle into the backseat. I'm not too keen on being in the back; it gives off this vibe like I'm somehow lording it over Omar. But he's got his study materials and snacks spread out on the passenger seat, and asking him to shift it all after keeping him waiting until ten in the evening doesn't sit right with me either.

"Good evening, Sir." I've given up asking him to call me Ben. Apparently it's against company policy. Both drivers are not directly employed by us because it's just easier to get them via a chauffeuring service as if one of them needs a day off they can send an alternative. But the downside is that they are not in our care, although Coop and I both insist that they get paid fairly.

"Can you take me straight home please?" I ask and swipe the screen of my phone nervously.

"No problem," he replies and puts the car in gear. As we roll out into the dark of the city, I finally tap the app.

Amelia

Hi Ben

She's replied! I take a deep breath. What now? I don't want to use the usual lines I throw to any other woman. She's not like them. She is Amelia.

My eyes fly over her profile.

CAT LADY WITH NO EXPERIENCE SEEKING HER MASTER.

Hm, think, Ben, think. Pick-up lines usually come easy to me. But then this situation is entirely different. I'm not trying to pick her up.

Me

> So, what brings a cat lady to the world of BDSM? Curiosity killed the cat…

Ok, great. If she doesn't know the proverb this will sound like a threat.

Amelia

> … But satisfaction brought it back.

Good girl. Of course she knows it.

Me

> Haha. So, what brings you here as a newbie?

Amelia

> "Friends" signed me up for it. I was very cross.

Me

> And yet you didn't delete the account.

She has always been an inquisitive soul, but the risk that she may end up with the wrong guy on here doesn't sit well with me. Especially as she's new to the community. There's a fire in my stomach again but it's not pleasant this time.

My gaze drifts to the world outside the car. Lights flash past as we make our way out of the city. I don't think I have ever had a bigger regret than when I messed things up with Amelia.

A ping from my phone alerts me to a new message.

Amelia

> Tbh my dating life hasn't been brilliant so I thought maybe this is what's been missing.

So many memories flood my brain. That was me, the not brilliant dating life. A disaster of a dating life more like. I should tell her who I am but I can't. Not yet.

4

All Or Nothing

Amelia

THE WATER SLOWLY CREEPS up to the bathtub's edge. I step out of my trousers, dropping them in the laundry basket on the way back to the bedroom where I grab my pyjamas from underneath my pillow. A tiny flashing light on my phone tells me I have another message.

I giggle nervously. So far that Ben guy hasn't said much, but he has at least not been weird like some of the other guys. I'm contemplating if I should take the phone with me when Smutty strolls into the bedroom and looks at me expectantly.

"No, no belly rubs for you now. I need a bath." He tries to stare me down, but I ignore him and head back to the bathroom with my phone held tightly in my hand. Who am I kidding? Not checking for messages was never an option.

As I walk past the full-length mirror, I catch a glimpse of myself. It's been a while since a man has seen my squishy bits. I casually treat my tummy to a gentle love tap. My belly gives me a wobble shuffle in response. I shrug. *I wonder if Ben likes his women thin or like me? No, no. You literally exchanged four messages with him.*

"Ah, Smutty, what would you think if I brought a guy with a whip home?" Smutty blinks at me in response and gives me a chirpy little meow.

Weirdly the image that comes to mind is not a certain Mr Grey but Indiana Jones. Ha, BDSM Indy, now that gives *Indiana Jones and the Temple of Doom* a completely different meaning.

I push through the initial pain and stinging sensation when my cold toes dip into the hot water and slide into the warmth. I swear I was a water nymph or a mermaid in my previous life. I could soak in a bath all day, until my fingers and toes resemble an ancient mummy's wrinkles.

Smutty plops himself on the bathmat and keeps a close eye on me. He despises water and always gets overprotective when I take a bath. *Silly cat.*

I reach for the hand towel hanging from the hook next to the sink and dry my hands before grabbing my phone. I hit the little message button on the dating app, making the first message pop up.

Wilfred

> I'm Lord Anal Pain and would like to explore your back passage.

Eww. I almost drop my phone into the water when trying to delete that message. *Lord Anal Pain. Seriously?*

But there is also a message from Ben.

Ben

> And what would "this" be that you missed from your dating life?

Before I can long think about it, my fingers fly over the keyboard typing out my reply.

Me

> I'm not sure. I've read a few BDSM romance novels and some of what is described in them is not really for me. And people that have contacted me so far are also a bit scary.

Ben

Does that include me?

Instant reply——that's a good sign, right?

Me

No!

I'm talking about Lord Anal Pain.

Me

No, you've been different.

Ben

Good. Happy to answer any questions about the community if you have any. Don't trust all you read in books or online.

Me

Okay. So, I googled pleasure dom. That's what you are. Right?

Ben

Yes. I've tried other areas in BDSM, but I found my niche as a pleasure dom.

Me

> So I read that you get pleasure from giving pleasure. Does that mean you don't spank?

Ben

> That depends on the submissive. If she enjoys spanking, I can provide that. But I don't get aroused from providing pain, it's the pleasure I provide to her that does it for me.

> Is that something that worries you? Spanking?

Me

> 100% I'm not really into spanking or pain.

I don't judge anyone who is, but I have bad associations with that and "sexy" really doesn't come to mind when I think about being hit.

Ben

> And you don't have to, if that's not something you're into. If anyone tells you otherwise, they are to be treated carefully. Consent is key.

Me

> You mean like Lord Anal Pain

Ben

WTF???

Me

That was my reaction when I thought I had a message from you and it was from the notorious L.A.P.

I hope he doesn't think I'm taking the mickey out of the BDSM scene.

Ben

Haha.

Just be careful with the app. There are a lot of genuine members on here who are looking for something (date, relationship) but there are also a ton of bellends who've watched too much bad porn and haven't got a clue.

Me

Noted.

Do you have a BDSM nickname?

Good lord, if this makes me blush then what the fuck am I doing on an app like this one?

Ben

No. I'm not playing a role. I'm me. My submissives tend to call me a term of respect. Some call me master, which, to be honest, is not my favourite, but I usually go with what she wants.

Me

I don't like master. Too... elite.

Ben

What would you call me?

Me

What?

Ben

Imagine it's just us two and you are doing as I tell you to. What would you call me to show me you are mine?

Fuck! I sink lower into the water. There's that tingling again. Imagining a strong guy above me. His big hand gently squeezing my throat asking me if I'm his good girl....

Me

Sir

My cheeks are burning and it's not from the steam in the bathroom. I realise that I've started to stroke my nipples with my free hand. *Flippin' heck, I'm a second away from sliding my fingers lower. All over some messages with a stranger who is probably pissing himself laughing about my naïve questions.*

Ben

Good girl.

Shit. In a panic I drop my mobile onto the soft bathmat next to the tub like it's a hot potato.

I sink into the warm water, letting it envelop me as I close my eyes and take a deep breath. I reach for the loofah to distract me from the feeling his messages left in me and squeeze some body wash onto it. As I begin to lather up, my mind starts to wander.

His profile did give away that he was tall and what was visible in his picture did hint that he probably works out. In my mind's eye, he has dark hair and piercing blue eyes. Not light blue, but dark like a sapphire.

A shiver runs down my spine as I recall his words. I'm insane to daydream anything into this given when we literally exchanged our first messages only an hour or so ago. But I can't help it. It's been so long since a man has paid me any attention. Or at least in a positive way. *Maybe I can convince him to teach me.* My heart starts beating a bit faster. *Yup, because I can do casual sex. That's never going to happen, Miss All or Nothing.*

I rinse off the suds from my body and set the loofah aside. Leaning back against the edge of the tub, I let my hands roam over my skin, tracing lazy circles along my thighs before moving higher to cup my breasts. *Ben.* That's always been one of my favourite names. I picture his strong hands exploring every inch of me with a hunger that matches my own. My nipples harden at the thought as I gently pinch them between my fingers. My hand continues its journey downward, gliding over my stomach until I get to my mound. I part my legs slightly and let out a soft moan as I make contact with my already swollen clit.

I start off slow, teasing myself with light strokes before applying more pressure. The sensation sends waves of pleasure coursing through me. *I need this.* As I continue to circle my clit with one hand, the other one moves lower until it finds its way inside me. I let out a gasp as I push two fingers in, my walls clenching around them.

"Sir," I whisper and that's all it takes to push me over the edge. I let out a soft moan, sapphire eyes still looking down at me. It's been a while since these eyes invaded my thoughts.

The room slowly comes back into focus. Smutty is staring at me in a very disapproving way.

"Wow," I whisper. Maybe that idea of being a submissive does appeal to me more than I thought.

"Don't you judge me," I point at Smutty, "I've seen you lick your own balls, Mister."

I finish washing myself before stepping out of the bath. There are butterflies in my tummy. Nervous butterflies and excited butterflies. *Fuck it, let's give this a try!*

F ORTY-FIVE MINUTES LATER I crawl under my duvet. That's how long I managed to draw my beauty regime out, and when I say beauty regime, I mean I put on face cream, brushed my teeth, and gave Smutty some belly rubs. Anything to not have to deal with reality and check the reply Ben sent me. *What if he turned from a nice guy into a creep? I mean, the internet is full of weirdos and perverts, right?*

My eyes zoom in on my phone on my nightstand. I grab it and then immediately put it back again. *Oh, for fuck's sake. It's not like he'll jump out of it.* I take a deep breath and swipe the screen.

Ben

> Well, let me know if you have any other questions.

Where to start? I have so many questions! But can I really send them through to a stranger? In the end, I decide to keep the door open for more.

Me

> Sorry, I had to get out of the bath. It's quite late, but I would love to continue our conversation another day?

Could I sound any more boring?

Ben

> Any time!

5

Believer

Ben

MY MUSCLES ARE STILL burning from my Saturday morning run. I pushed myself a lot harder than I usually would, but when my mind is racing, my body needs to move.

Yesterday evening was tense, especially when Amelia left me hanging for nearly an hour after my *Good Girl* comment. I thought I'd blown it. When she finally got back in touch I was close to losing my mind.

The washing machine beeps happily at me after I press the start button. I have a housekeeper Monday to Friday who does my washing and cleans my house, but if I keep my sweaty running clothes for the whole weekend to be washed on Monday they'll stink to high heaven and I really can't do that to Gustavo.

My fingers run through my hair which is still damp from the shower as I make my way back to the smoothie I have chilling in the fridge. The small utility room on the ground floor is just off the kitchen. There's also a decent-sized living room with an adjacent office that pulls double duty as my personal library. Upstairs there are three bedrooms. Do I actually need that many? Not really. But I loved the garden when I first viewed the house. And it's right next door to my sister's place. That and the amazing view of the fields surrounding the village sold me on it. Sure, with the success our company has had, I could easily afford something even bigger. But who wants all those empty rooms?

I swallow the last of the green sludge that is sold as a "healthy smoothie" when someone rings the doorbell over and over. I can't stop a grin from forming on my lips. My favourite little munchkin is here. I place my glass in the sink and head to the front door.

"Do I know you?" I ask as seriously as I can muster.

"Uncle Ben, it's me, silly," a cheeky five-year-old grins at me. His front top two teeth are missing and his little tongue pokes through the gap.

"And who are you?" I ask again and bend down like I'm inspecting him closely.

"Robbie," he sighs exasperated.

"Oh, Robbie. I think I have a nephew called Robbie," I grin making him chuckle.

"Yup, me."

"That's yes, not yup," my sister Fiona, who has been watching us, corrects him.

"Yes, me," Robbie repeats pointing his little fingers at himself.

"Well, if you are really my nephew I think you should give me a hug!" I haven't finished the sentence when the little squirt jumps into my arms. He has the same blond hair and green eyes as Fi. She and I couldn't be more different. Fi is short, petite and fair. Aside from towering over her, I have the broody dark look that women usually flock to like moths to a flame. But we are as similar in character as we are different in looks. We are both driven people who know what we want. In her case, that was being the best mum anyone could imagine. Her older kids, Sam and Claire, are both at university, and then five years ago Robbie joined the family as a surprise. Fi struggled at the beginning, having mentally prepared herself for an empty nest with her teenagers gone. But luckily, she has a husband who couldn't have been more supportive. Once

Robbie was born everyone doted on him. And the little munchkin knows it. He has us all in his tiny palm.

"How are you, Robster?" I ask him, placing a kiss on my sister's cheek. Robbie slides his hand in mine as we walk into the kitchen. Saturdays he and Fi usually come over for lunch whilst my brother-in-law plays football for the village team. Robbie hates football, something nobody in the family understands. We are an Aston Villa family, my dad made sure of that. We all love football. Except for the little squirt.

"I'm hungry," Robbie grins at me. Of course he is. He has the energy of ten kids and runs around all day long. But he also has the appetite of ten of these little monsters.

"Well, it's a good thing that I have lunch almost ready then," I chuckle. The pasta sauce has been bubbling away in the slow cooker whilst I was out for my run.

"And dessert?"

"And dessert. But only if you eat all of your spaghetti." I reply. I've been told off by my sister more than once for giving him dessert too easily and now I always make sure he gets his proper food first. He hates vegetables, so the whole family has mastered sneaking them into food he will eat. Spaghetti Bolognese is his favourite and the perfect decoy. He has yet to find out. *Did I mention that he rules with an iron fist?*

"Okay," Robbie agrees, probably because it is spaghetti. "Can I play outside?" I built a large slide and climbing frame in my garden for him and he loves it.

"But only until lunch. It's cold today," Fi says but before she finishes the sentence he's already sprinting to the back-door.

"Tea?" I hold up the kettle.

"Oh, that would be amazing," Fi sighs as she slides onto the little stool next to the breakfast bar.

"Tough week?" I ask with a frown. Fi sometimes does too much and doesn't allow herself a break.

"Not more than usual," she waves me off. That's her signal to me to let it go. She doesn't want to talk about it.

"Guess what?" I change the topic. I have to tell someone about Amelia. The only people that know what I went through back then are my family and Coop.

"You're going to let Robbie move in with you?" she asks as she gets up again, fetches milk from the fridge and hands it over to me.

I know she is just joking, but I remind myself to make more time to watch Robbie and take some pressure off her.

"Funny, but no. I ran into Amelia."

"Amelia... the Amelia? The one whose heart you broke?" I flinch at her words. "Sorry," she adds and gives my arm a pat. She isn't wrong but it's also not quite that simple.

"Yes, that Amelia."

"Where did you meet her? I know she still lives in the village, but in all these years I haven't so much as caught a glimpse of her." Fi asks as she stirs her tea .

"Uncle Ben, look!" Robbie shouts from the garden and we both direct our eyes to him. I wave and he waves back before coasting down the slide.

"I stumbled across her profile on a dating app." No need to explain which app exactly.

My sister knows that I'm into BDSM. We had to have the world's most embarrassing conversation when she and I had dinner one evening and Gina decided to surprise me. I was in the bathroom, so my sister opened the front door to a woman with her coat open and not much else underneath, purring "Time for my spanking, Master." But it's not something we talk about, and I definitely haven't told her that I'm a pleasure dom. Imagine that admission over Sunday roast.

"And?" she asks, taking another sip of her tea.

"I messaged her, but I didn't tell her it's me."

"You're catfishing her?"

"No! It's my name, my details, but my photo only shows me up to here." I hold my hand at nose height. "I just didn't tell her that it's me."

"Ben. What do you think is going to happen when she finds out?" She gives me a dark look.

"I don't know. But if I tell her now, she'll just block me again. I need a chance to explain."

"Ben—"

"Fi, I need this chance. I need to see her. I need to talk to her. I need to apologise." There is desperation in my voice. I rub the back of my neck nervously.

"You guys broke up such a long time ago. Are you still hung up on her? I thought you'd moved on. You never speak about her." Fi studies my face.

"It's not that. I just want a chance to apologise," I defend myself.

"Ben, it's been years. Isn't it water under the bridge by now?"

"It's never too late," I sigh, my gaze drifting to the garden where Robbie is swinging from the monkey bars. "Never too late to apologise."

"So, what did she say in the app?"

"Oh, we just had a casual conversation." I grin and hope she'll let it go because I really can't tell her what we talked about.

"At least do me a favour and set your expectations low. I remember what a mess you were after she broke up with you." There is genuine concern in her voice.

"I'm just going to apologise."

A KNOCK ON MY door draws my attention away from my computer, but before I can reply, it's pulled open. I don't need to check who it is. Only one person would enter my office before I invite them in. Coop gives me a grin and plonks himself into the chair in front of my desk.

"If you are here to gloat that you're taking a beautiful woman on a romantic trip, you can fuck off," I smirk.

"No gloating. And it's not just a romantic trip." He places a small ring box on my desk.

"Ah, that's so sweet, but you're are not my type so no, I won't marry you." I chuckle.

"Wanker," he laughs.

"Are you sure you are ready?" I ask more seriously. I feel as a friend it's my duty to ask him, even if I know he's doing the right thing. He and Lizzie are meant for each other.

"One thousand percent sure." He has a dopey look on his face.

"In which case I approve. Congratulations, mate."

"Thanks. But she hasn't said yes yet." Could he genuinely be worried she might say no? I lean back in my chair and cross my arms.

"Don't be stupid, Coop. Lizzie adores you." He just shrugs before taking the ring box and placing it back in his pocket.

"There's something else, Ben."

"Yes, I'll be your best man," I grin. Coop just rolls his eyes.

"I'm serious. I want us to hire a general manager." My smile drops.

"What? Why?"

"Why? Because I don't want to work such long hours anymore and I don't want for you to, either. We have both worked our socks off for the last fifteen years. It's time to enjoy our hard work. We'll still be involved. Joined Executive Directors, just like now. All major decisions will be made by us and we'll have full oversight, but we don't have to deal with the day-to-day stuff anymore."

Our company, M&W, holds subsidiaries operating in different trades. We have three tech companies developing new gadgets and a large construction company specialising in high rise buildings. There are a number of smaller businesses, but all our endeavours are about innovation . We've made a name for ourselves by being fair trading partners who are tough at the negotiation table but reliable in the delivery of high-quality products. Our big break came when we snapped up a project for the Olympic Games.

After that success, Coop and I agreed to stop further expansion. No more new acquisitions. Instead, we're building our brand with a focus on reliability and advancement. We both have more money than we could ever want and there's no need to be greedy. That's why I really shouldn't be surprised by Coop's suggestion regarding a general manager.

"I don't know, Coop—"

"Think about it, that's all I ask. We'll talk about it when I'm back. We'll only do it if we both agree to it." He's serious and the thought of slowing down a bit does sound more than appealing. But what do I slow down for?

A ping pulls me from my thoughts. I turn my phone around and see a message from Amelia.

Amelia

Okay, I may have some more questions.

Is now a good time?

There's a knock on my door but I ignore it.

"Come in," Coop calls out. My eyes are trained on my phone.

Me

> I told you. Any time. What questions do you have?

"Hey, Ben." Lizzie grins at me.

"Hey, Giggles and Laughter," I smirk.

"Oh my god, can you cut it out?" Lizzie protests before kissing Coop. "It's been over fifteen years."

"Yeah, but it's still the most ridiculous answer I've ever been given in a job interview." I chuckle. It was definitely an interview I'll never forget. Not only did she turn up late, she also said the most absurd things. I asked her what her strengths were and she said *giggles and laughter*. Hence my nickname for her. The only thing Coop and I agreed on at the end was that we wouldn't hire her. I thought she was a tiny bit nuts——to be honest, I still think she is a bit nuts, but in a good way. Coop thought she was adorable, though not meant for that job. They became good friends and the rest is history.

Coop and Lizzie start their usually flirty bickering which allows me to ignore them for a few moments.

Amelia

> How do you ask someone to be your pleasure dom?

I take a deep breath and my heart rate increases. Is she asking hypothetically or is she asking me? Another ping.

Amelia

> My Cat was wondering.

> Oh, that sounded funnier in my head.

A small smile appears on my lips.

"What the fuck is going on?" Coop chuckles and brings me back to the room.

"Nothing," I reply, but I can't wipe the grin of my face.

"Who is she?" Lizzie probes with a knowing smirk.

"A cat lady," is the only answer I give her. "But you two bugger off on your holiday. How many suitcases do you have this time, Giggles?"

Lizzie gives me an evil look. "One!"

"Well, off you go. Have a good time in Canada and don't freeze your toes or other extremities off," I laugh.

Lizzie keeps probing me about the message, but over my dead body will I mention Amelia's name just as they are about to leave on a two-week holiday. Nobody knows more about what happened than Coop, and he would worry the whole time they are away. I can't let that happen.

Eventually, I manage to usher them out of the office. I relax back in my chair and start to type a reply to Amelia.

Me

> Is your pussy cat looking for a plea-sure dom?

I hold my breath until the next message appears.

Amelia

> Maybe. :-)

My fingers fly over the screen.

Me

> Well, you can attend workshops in the scene or forums to meet people. Or you can join apps like this one. Sorry, your pussy cat can ;-)

Amelia

> And once you've found one?

Me

> You get to know each other a little and then meet up, like with any dating really. I usually meet people in a public place like a pub or restaurant first so we both feel comfortable. I mean, I told you that there are some shady characters on this app.

Amelia

> Why do you hide your face in your profile?

Fair question, I guess, and I knew it would come at some point.

Me

> I have my own business and some of the people I do business with and their wives are on here. I don't need anyone to know about my private life.

Amelia

> Oh shit. I didn't even think about work. :-O

I grin to myself. *Luckily!* Otherwise, I may not have known it's her.

Amelia

> Fixed it :-)

I press a few buttons on my screen and Amelia's profile pops up. It is now a close up of her cat and she is no longer visible.

Me

> So now you have a pussy as a profile picture LOL

Amelia

> Oh. :-0

What I would give to see her now! I gaze out of the large window at the city. This nagging sense of guilt is getting stronger and stronger the longer we chat . I've got to come clean about who I am. I need to. The more I delay it, the worse it's going to be when we finally meet.

Me

> Can I ask you something?

Amelia

> Sure

Me

> Do you want to have dinner with me?

6

Gimme! Gimme! Gimme! (A Man After Midnight)

Amelia

THE SMELL IN THE ladies toilet is pungent to say the least. Our office is not in the nicest building and the bathrooms are shared with other companies on our floor. As with most communal spaces, nobody bothers keeping them nice and tidy. I try not to breathe through my nose when I enter the first cubicle. Samira positions herself outside with my washbag and a new top in hand.

"I still can't believe you're meeting with this guy. What if he ties you up and spanks you?" she whisper-shouts and giggles.

"In the middle of a restaurant?" I reply without admitting that I have had that thought a few times as well. "Besides, he's a pleasure dom," I mumble under my breath as I pull my cardigan and T-shirt over my head.

"Right, he only cares about your pleasure. Sounds like a pickup line to me. When have you ever met a man that cares about your pleasure first?" she argues and there's a thud on the door. I hold out my hand over the top of the cubicle and Samira presses the silky material of the top I ordered earlier this week into my hand.

Fine, yes, I ordered a new outfit for this date, but my wardrobe almost entirely consists of black or grey T-shirts and muted coloured cardigans. I have to make an effort, right?

"Well, I googled it and everything he said matches what I read online." The blue top slides over my body and fans out over my hips. I stare down at my breasts that are quite prominent in this outfit. The top is low cut and the new bra is lifting my big boobs up making them almost jump out of the top.

"I can't wear this," I sigh.

"Why?" Samira replies. "Let me see!" I unlock the cubicle and open the door a little so she can peek through the gap.

"My bra is showing." I point where a little bit of lace is sticking out from underneath the collar.

"This is why you have these." She wedges my toiletry bag between her knees and holds up a packet of little strips. She peels off the protective layer on one side of the strip and sticks it to the exposed skin on the top of my boob. Then she fiddles with the remaining protective layer of the double-sided tape, pulls my top up a little and smashes it onto the sticky side. The material of the top now sticks to my boob. For how long though, that is another question .

"Now do the same on the other side," she demands and pushes me back into the cubicle.

"For someone who isn't sure if I should meet this guy you are pushing quite hard," I giggle.

"Hey, I'm just glad you're getting yourself out there for once. Maybe when the pleasure man turns out to be a weirdo you'll run into your prince charming who'll rescue you."

"Are we still getting rescued in this day and age?" I retort, ripping off the sticky strip I had just placed on my breast because it was too high. "Fuck!" I swear loudly. This was almost more painful than when I once ripped my eyebrow off with a peel off mask... by mistake.

"There's nothing wrong with accepting help." Samira's voice comes from further away.

It's fiddlier than I thought, but eventually I get the double-sided tape in place and the other side of my top is also secured to my breast. When I open the cubicle door, Samira inspects me from head to toe.

"You look amazing," she grins.

"Let's not exaggerate. I look okay, I guess," I catch sight of myself in the mirror. The top is more form fitting than what I normally wear. A belt is cinching it in the waist, giving me kind of an hourglass figure. A big hourglass, that is.

"No, you look beautiful. And don't forget, he's seen what you look like. He's the one that is hiding half his face. I mean, he might have a monobrow." She crunches up her nose.

I laugh, " You know what, I'm not sure I'd care. He's nice."

"He could have a Satan tattoo on his forehead," she muses. "Or be bald."

"No, you can see some of his hair in the picture," I giggle.

"Just promise me you'll be careful and you'll keep texting me so I know he hasn't dragged you off to his dungeon," she says with genuine concern in her voice. I grab my toiletry bag from her hands and take out a brush.

"Sure," I promise as I bend over and awkwardly try to blow dry my fringe with the hand dryer. I have a natural wave to my hair and after a day in the office my fringe sticks in all directions.

I pull out some of the makeup I bought on my lunch break and start painting it on. I don't usually wear makeup, just some mascara, but the last thing a pleasure dom will be interested in is a plain Jane.

"Wow, you look like... I don't know—" Samira is staring at me in the mirror. I can see her biting her lips. Yes, I look ridiculous. I don't look like me.

"I look like a drag queen," I sigh.

"Maybe a tiny bit," Samira giggles.

"Oh fuck it," I grab a face wipe and take all the makeup off again before putting some mascara on. *There, that's me. Take it or leave it Ben.*

I T'S TEN TO FIVE. *That's not too early. That's not too eager, right?* I walk into the restaurant which is still fairly quiet this early in the evening. My eyes scan the room, although I'm not sure why. I don't know what he looks like. "I'll find you," he said. *Oh, he is so going to ghost me.*

My eyes move from table to table. Then I freeze. *Fuck. What is he doing here?* A hot flash shoots through me. I'm not sure if it is residual anger or sheer panic. I ought to avert my gaze, but he's caught my eye, and I just can't tear myself away. Panic wells up in me. There, at the far end of the restaurant, sits the man who broke my heart so thoroughly that it messed me up for years. Benjamin Whitmore. I haven't seen him since that fateful day almost twenty years ago and I had hoped to never see him again in my life. I was good at avoiding him even when we lived in the same village.

I know his sister still lives in Little Hadlow but I haven't spoken to her in years. It's a small village but it's big enough to avoid people you don't want to meet. I occasionally spot her from the distance, but I have a spidey sense for the Whitmores and I hotfoot it in the other direction when I see any of them. I can't possibly face her, or Ben, after everything that happened. Who needs that awkwardness?

Luckily, Ben moved to the US a year after we broke up and he's barely been home since. And I haven't thought about him in the last few years. Not often, at least.

I should turn around and walk away but what would Ben think if I stood him up? If he turns up, that is.

Ben! Suddenly something clicks in my brain. *No, no, no.* Heat creeps into my cheeks and a sense of doom settles in my guts.

That bastard! Ben Whitmore is *my* Ben. Pleasure Dom Ben is the person who ripped my heart out and stamped on it. Looks like my spidey sense doesn't work online.

Before I can leave, he gets out of the little booth and walks up to me.

"Hi, Amelia."

"You... You—" Bastard. Rat. Arsehole. Smoking hot heart-breaker. No, forget smoking hot.

"Please, Amelia! Don't run. Give me a chance to expla in... Just one dinner. Please," he begs. There are laughter lines on his face and some grey in his hair and his stubble. It makes him look more manly, distinguished, and hot. *No, not hot, I said! Don't even go there!*

But his eyes themselves haven't changed. They are a cool shade of blue, like a sapphire. Long, dark lashes frame them. I always loved his eyes and I'm still convinced it was his eyes that bewitched me, all these years back.

I look around the quiet restaurant, unsure of what to do. My gut feeling tells me I should run, I should get away from him. He broke me once and judging by the messages we've exchanged so far, he could break me again. But something is stopping me. It has been a long time and we have never spoken about what happened, simply because I didn't give him a chance.

What is there to explain if someone——no, not someone: your boyfriend——laughs about you behind your back and calls you ugly?

I wait for the angry fire to start in my chest. The one that I felt alongside the sadness of losing him. But nothing.

I always wondered why he did it. Why did he go out with me if that was his opinion of me? Maybe it's time to face my fear and hear him out?

"Please," he whispers and he looks nervous. "I know I should have told you that it's me you've been chatting with but I was scared you'd block me and I want nothing more than to finally explain what happened." He's showing vulnerability I've never seen in him.

His eyes bore into me and butterflies, knots... something is forming in my stomach. The door behind me opens and I realise we're blocking the entrance. My eyes fall shut as I take a deep breath. Maybe when I open them, this will all have been a bad dream. Ben's hand on my arm, gently pulling me to the side so the people stepping into the restaurant behind me can pass, brings me back.

It wasn't a dream or a nightmare. Ben Whitmore is still looking at me with pleading puppy eyes.

"Okay, fine," I finally exhale, "But only because I'm hungry." I lift my chin in defiance, pretending his presence hasn't set off a firework of emotions in me.

"Thank you." His deep and silky voice sends a shiver through me, but I try desperately not to show it.

"Just promise me you'll give it to me straight. Don't lie to me," I mumble.

"I never lied," he replies defiantly.

"Ha," I laugh bitterly because, right there, this was a lie. A big fat fucking lie.

As we head to the table, I send Samira the promised text to make sure she doesn't alert the special forces to rescue me.

Me

Don't worry. Turns out Ben and I know each other from when we were young. I'll tell you everything when you're back from your holiday. XX

7

Crash! Boom! Bang!

Amelia

*B*EN IS DRAGGING ME *along empty streets. The sun is relentless and I feel sweat on my forehead. We're on the way to his colleague Ian's house to watch the England game. Frankly I would have preferred to hide in an air-conditioned coffee shop with a book.*

"Tell me again why I need to come?" I ask. I hate his new work colleagues. His Uni friend Cooper is a lot more my cup of tea. He's kind.

Ben started at this investment company six months ago and ever since his whole life revolves around his job and his coworkers . I've met them a couple of times and I find them rude and superficial. Ben is a different person when he is with them. When it's just the two of us, he's loving and caring, and makes me laugh to the point that I wonder how I got so lucky. But around them he changes, roaring along with their crude jokes and basically ignoring me.

"Because I want to spend time with you but I need to show my face at this thing. If I want to get a promotion in the autumn my boss needs to see me at work things." Ben stops and pulls me into his arms, placing a soft kiss on my forehead.

"It's watching the footie, not really a work thing," I protest.

"Amelia," he sighs. "Please? For me? We don't have to stay long."

"Fine," I giggle. "But only because you have a cute bum." Ben lets out a deep belly laugh before drawing me into a passionate kiss.

Honestly, I would do anything for him when he kisses me like that.

*I*AN DOES HAVE A *nice house, I have to give him that. Walking from the toilet through his large living room back to the garden I notice all the details that have gone into the decor. I bet he hired someone to decorate it for him.*

As I step back outside, I freeze in my tracks when the sound of my name reaches my ears. The trellis overgrown with vines shield me from view.

"Seriously, mate. I don't know why you're with Amelia."

"Well, I guess she isn't what people would consider pretty ..." Ben's words hit me like a ton of bricks. I find it difficult to breathe. I hear him chuckle nervously. I know his laugh and that is not his normal one.

Ian chimes in, "But, mate, you can do so much better."

"Maybe you're right, but she is extra appreciative for my attention , if you know what I mean." His statement makes them all whoop and laugh.

"And until someone better comes along, I'll enjoy it, lads," Ben adds, sparking more laughter. His hurtful remarks cut through me. Is that really what he thinks? Has it all been a lie? My heart races as I try to make sense of it all. He told me at least twenty times that he loved me only yesterday. We cooked pasta together and ended up in a food fight and then had some incredible kitchen-counter sex. I feel sick to my stomach when I think that he faked it all.

I need to get out of here. I don't want to hear anything else. I'm fighting with tears. Don't cry, don't cry, don't cry.

Taking a step back, I accidentally bump into someone —Adam— another one of Ben's so-called friends. His awkward grin makes it clear he also heard the conversation. My embarrassment and hurt mix into a cocktail of emotions and I just want to run. I need to get out of here.

"Can you tell Ben I've left?" I ask Adam in a hushed tone, not bothering to wait for a reply. I make my way through the living room and out the front door. Ian doesn't live too far from station, I can get a train home from there.

"Breathe, breathe, breathe," I mumble to myself, trying to calm my emotions. Anger, humiliation, and a deep sadness swirl together, the sadness slowly becoming overwhelming .

I hear my name shouted as I'm about to round the corner, and see Ben running towards me. Catching up, he tentatively touches my arm and says my name again. My stomach tightens and I force myself to turn, mustering a strained smile. Confusion and worry paint his face, mirroring how I feel inside.

"I'm sorry, I can explain," he starts, but turn back towards the station building in the distance. He grabs my hand, desperate to stop me from leaving. I pull from his grasp like his touch burns me.

"Please don't go, let me explain, I didn't—" he pleads, but I silence him with a hand over his mouth. Hurt and disappointment are like a knot in my chest.

"I get it. And I agree," I assert. He shakes his head, struggling to process my composed response. I force another smile and add, "I've been telling you from day one that you can do so much better than me. And I hope you find it. Truly. Just a tip, don't lie in your next relationship. Lies always come out. Always."

He looks at me, stunned and confused. He doesn't seem to understand what's happening. He probably expected tears, shouting, or even a punch to the stomach. I don't know if my reactions come from not wanting to show him how much he is hurting me or because I genuinely agree with him. He can do better than me. I mean, the only thing separating me from being a cat lady is a cat. He, on the other hand, is hot, smart, funny, driven... He's the full package. Aside from being a liar, that is.

While he fumbles for words, I walk off.

"Amelia!"

I turn one more time, "No, Ben. Let's leave it. Please don't follow me. And please don't contact me anymore." I continue walking and don't look back but the weight of the moment lingers in the air. With every step away from him my heart breaks a little more and I have to stop myself from turning around and begging him to take me back. Then my inner voice takes over and convinces me that of course someone like Ben won't stay with me.

"Let him go, Amelia. You were not meant to be," I whisper to myself. I just wish my heart would accept the facts as easily as my brain. It's that pesky optimism that's waiting for him to come after me, that keeps telling my heart that maybe... No! Enough! There is no maybe. I just lost the love of my life.

8

You Are The Reason

Ben

A MELIA SLIDES INTO THE booth and rips the menu from the waiter's hand. He gives her a scared look, and she realises she's taking out her anger on him. She apologises in a hushed tone before burying her face in the menu.

I want to slide next to her but think better of it and take a seat on the other side of the table. I can live with every emotion she wants to throw at me. Anger, frustration, hate, fury, anything as long as she doesn't walk away from me again.

I allow myself to study her whilst her attention is on the menu. Even in her fury she looks beautiful. Her features are still as gentle and warm as they were so many years ago. There are now some faint lines around her eyes and the corners of her mouth, and they bring me joy because it tells me she's had plenty of opportunities to laugh. Her hair is still the same shade of gold, triggering memories of how soft it felt when I ran my fingers through it. Her curves are the same curves I used to love tracing with my fingers. She is still as breath-taking as she was so many years ago.

I clear my throat and lower my gaze, trying to focus on the menu. No good can come from that train of thought. *You're just here to apologise.*

Neither of us say anything until the waiter has taken our order. With the menus gone there is nowhere to hide. Not for her and not for me. Amelia fiddles nervously with the cutlery in front of her.

"I'm sorry, Amelia." I break the silence and finally her eyes find mine.

"For what?" There is a coldness to her voice which I definitely deserve. "For lying to me when you pretended to be in love with me, or for lying to me when you pretended to be someone you weren't?"

"Neither," I reply and take a sip of my water. Amelia snorts bitterly.

"I loved you. I never lied about that. Neither did I pretend I was someone I wasn't. I'm Ben, I'm a pleasure dom, I was on the app to find someone to meet up with, came across your profile and reached out to you. I keep my face out of pictures because of my business. That's it. I withheld some information, but I didn't lie."

Amelia shakes her head before locking eyes with me again, "Then what are you sorry about, Ben? What? And no bullshit."

Over the years I've had this conversation in my head so many times, but now that I have the chance to explain what happened it all sounds stupid.

"I'm sorry for..., I'm sorry that I was such a wanker back then," I sigh. "I let myself get sucked into this superficial world and I wanted to fit in with the other guys. I couldn't see what arseholes they were. I said and did things when I was with them that I'm deeply ashamed of now. Not to mention that I did some business deals that weren't quite illegal, but definitely immoral. Success was judged by who could make the most money by any means possible, and I was blinded by it."

I study her face but I can't read her emotions.

"There's no excuse for what I said at Ian's back then. None at all. As I said the words out loud I was shouting at myself inside for being such an arsehole, especially because I didn't mean them. I was in love with you. I was crazy about you, but I was also a power-hungry twat who wanted to get ahead."

"And now you want me to forgive you?" Her voice sounds calmer, but I'm not sure if this is better than her anger.

"No," I wince. "I don't think I have the right to ask that from you. Not after just one dinner. I hope one day you can trust that I'm not that man anymore and you can truly forgive me, but no, I won't ask you to forgive me today."

"So, what do you want, Ben?"

"A chance to become your friend and prove to you that I've changed."

"You want to be my friend?"

"Yes. I've moved back to Little Hadlow. I'm invited to Miranda's wedding. It's going to be difficult to avoid each other forever."

"I can say hello when I pass you in the street," she replies, stubbornly avoiding my point.

"Amelia." I wait until her eyes are on me. "You know that's not what I meant."

"I don't know. I'm confused. I should sit here and be angry with you for what you did all these years ago, but that kind of feels like a distant memory. I remember the pain, but it's pain from the past. Doesn't mean I've forgiven you, but at least it doesn't hurt anymore. Maybe because I lived with it long enough."

Her words hit me right in the chest and I swallow hard.

"I do feel angry though for... for not telling me who you are; I mean my old Ben. I mean, I came here thinking I may—" Her cheeks flush red and she takes a sip from her water.

"You were hoping to shag a pleasure dom?" I ask outright and Amelia chokes on her water. The fact that the waiter arrived exactly at that time with our food and stares at us with big eyes doesn't help Amelia's embarrassment. I have to bite my lip to not grin at her.

"What the fuck?" she hisses at me once the waiter walks away.

"Am I wrong?"

"Well,—" she blushes a little more and takes a bite of her steak. "What have you been up to for all these years?" she changes the topic.

"After you walked away from me I fell into an emotional black hole. I wanted to force you to listen to me, but Coop stopped me. Do you remember Cooper?"

"Of course I do. He was nice. Why did he stop you?" Is that disappointment in her voice?

"Because I was a wanker and I didn't deserve you. I almost lost him as a best friend as well. He told me he wouldn't hang out with me until I ditched the arseholes." I take a bite of my food.

"And you did?" she asks, surprise showing on her face.

"I thought I needed these guys to grow at work. But I started to question things after you walked away from me and Coop almost did the same. I realised I needed to leave all that behind and grow up. In the end I resigned. Coop's dad helped us set up our first company; it was a small start-up but we put our everything into it. After a year we opened an office in New York and decided that I would run that location whilst Coop would manage the London office. We then kept opening branches around the world and it was usually me who would man the new office until it was up and running with New York as my base." I settle back into my seat, finding it comforting to talk to her almost as if no time has passed at all.

"But in the last couple of years I just became really homesick. I missed my family. I missed out on so many family events and on seeing my niece and nephews growing up. And so I came back. Our company is successful enough now that we can easily run it from London because we have good people in charge of all our subsidiaries." I shrug.

"How's Coop?" she asks between bites.

I smile, "He's good. He and his best friend are about to get engaged."

"Oh, congratulations to you and Coop," Amelia chuckles. For a moment the mood feels light-hearted.

"Funny," I grin, "I'm his best guy friend. He and Lizzie met not long after we set up our company when she applied for a job with us. She didn't get the job, but they became best friends."

"And then?" Amelia leans forward, her eyes sparkling. She's always been a romantic.

I mime zipping my lips. "That's Coop's story. Join us for lunch soon and he can tell you."

"Ben—" she sighs heavily and leans back, pushing the food on her plate around. My heart drops. *Did I go too far?*

"It would be nice to see Coop though," she finally says and gives me a small smile that doesn't quite reach her eyes. I feel a little relief but I'm still on edge.

"So how about you?"

"Hm?" Her eyes look sad when she turns them to me.

"What have you been up to?"

"Nothing half as exciting as you. I worked as administrator for many years. Eventually I moved into the charity sector and did some courses on security and risk. I'm now the Head of Security Risk Management for a tech company providing communication tools to aid agencies in the field."

"That doesn't sound like nothing." I smile, but she gives me an embarrassed look. She was never good with compliments. "Ever been married?" I ask casually but the minute the words leave my lips, I wish I could take them back. Somehow it feels like I'm bringing us back to dangerous territory.

"Not even close," she replies with a blank expression. "I was in a couple of relationships but they were guys I wasn't really in love with. The guys I'm interested in aren't usually interested in me and—" She bites her lip as if she's said too much.

"I'm sorry." *What am I sorry for?* For asking the question? For bringing up memories? Or is it just another sorry for hurting her so badly? Regardless, she lets it go this time.

"When did you become a pleasure dom?" she suddenly whispers. Her cheeks turn crimson again despite the interest in her eyes.

"When I moved to the US I started dating a woman who was in the BDSM scene. She introduced me, and I guess you could say instructed me. I tested the waters for a few years and tried out different things until I discovered what it means to be a pleasure dom. It all made a lot more sense to me and I felt I'd found myself."

"And I guess a pleasure dom doesn't get married?" she giggles.

"Why not?"

"Oh, you are married?"

"No," I chuckle as I see something in her eyes that looks an awful lot like jealousy, "but it doesn't mean I can't get married. Being a pleasure dom isn't my life, it's part of my life. It's how I like to have sex, nothing else."

"Oh, okay." She doesn't look convinced.

"Amelia, forget what you may have seen in movies." I reach out and place my hand on top of hers. She freezes for a moment and then slowly pulls her hand from mine.

"So, you have to be in love with someone to be a PD?"

"Police Detective?" I laugh.

"Ben." She playfully slaps my arm.

"No, I don't have to be in love. You can have sex without being in love or it can be part of a loving relationship. That's the same with being a pleasure dom." I pronounce the last two words loudly, and Amelia shyly looks around to see if anyone else heard. *Fuck, she's adorable.*

9

Hungry Eyes

Amelia

OKAY, THAT ESCALATED QUICKLY.

"Let's talk about something else." I take another sip of my water. I would love to press the cool glass against my cheeks because I can feel them burning but we're in a posh place, and I don't even want to know what the waiter already thinks of us.

"You did come here for that." He gives me a cheeky smile.

"Yes, when I thought you were someone completely different." My words wipe the smirk off his face.

"Amelia, I—"

"It's fine. Well, fine might be strong, but I get it. You're right, I wouldn't have come if I'd known it was you. And I'm kind of glad I did." I genuinely am. It's definitely better than if I'd run into him for the first time at Miranda's wedding. At least we've had a chance to clear the air, and I wasn't lying earlier when I said that I didn't really feel any anger for what happened so long ago. I'm surprised about that myself. I guess time does heal all.

"I'm glad too." He wipes his mouth with his napkin before placing it on top of his empty plate. "And my offer stands, if you have any questions about PD I'm happy to answer them."

Heat shoots through me again. *For heaven's sake.* How can I ever hope to go ahead with trying out a submissive role if the simple mention of it makes me go red like a tomato?

"I don't think that's a good idea," I mumble and reach for my glass only to find it empty.

"Why not? I mean, maybe I shouldn't point this out, but we've seen each other naked before." He fills my glass from the water jug before topping up his own.

"So?" I take a big gulp of water. This conversation is making me feel nervous.

"So, surely that should take some embarrassment out of the situation compared to asking a stranger." There is some logic in that I'm sure, but in this moment it sounds utterly ridiculous.

"I can't sleep with you!" I hiss. For a brief second he looks alarmed but then has his expression under control again.

"Darling... Amelia, that's not what I'm suggesting." Darling? He has never called me "darling" before.

"I'm just saying that if you have questions I'm here to answer them."

I study his face. His expression is neutral but there is something in his eyes. Something I can't read, but that intrigues me nevertheless.

"And if I want more?" The devil knows what has come over me. I'm not really contemplating sleeping with him but I want to see that panic again. My words hit the bullseye, and he gives me the same look as a few minutes ago.

"Then I would agree, as long as we set some rules."

"Bullshit," I exclaim which earns me some curious looks from another table close by. "Bullshit," I repeat in a muted tone, "I saw the panic in your eyes. You're lying again."

"No, I'm not. But you're right. The thought does scare me." His voice is soft. He no longer has the puppy dog enthusiasm he had when we were younger. Back then, he would go after every idea he had with passion. Now he seems to be more grounded, weighing up both sides of a coin.

"What scares you about it?"

"I'm not sure we could leave the emotional baggage behind us. Even if we're not in love I would need you to trust me, and the question is if you could do that given how much I hurt you ." *Oh wow.* He's showing more vulnerability and honesty than I expected.

"Maybe you're right. But then, this experiment was never about emotions and I do trust that you would never hurt me ...physically. That much I know." My fingers keep stroking over the napkin as if they want to flatten out all creases. "But, let's not talk about it. It's irrelevant because we're not doing that ."

Ben is silent for a second before agreeing, "No, of course not."

"No." Our eyes meet and my heart is beating a little faster.

"Right, do you want dessert?" He knows I have a sweet tooth and my very obvious squishy bits show that this hasn't changed.

"No. Thank you. I should get home." There is disappointment on his face for a second but he waves the waiter over and asks for the bill.

"Let me at least give you a lift back to Little Hadlow."

"That's not necessary," I object. The thought of sitting in a car with him for another hour makes me feel nervous.

"Don't be silly, Amelia. I have a driver who will take me home and we live in the same village." He's right. It would be ridiculous for me to take the train when we're going to the same place.

"Fine," I finally agree and place my debit card next to his on the little tray with the bill .

"No, Amelia—"

"Yes, Ben. This wasn't a date. I'll pay my half." I can see he wants to disagree but in the end he doesn't. Apparently he hasn't completely changed.

I'M SITTING ON MY bed phone in hand, staring at the number I'm about to call. Ben's number. I take a deep breath and press the call button before I can chicken out.

It's been a week since our dinner. On the drive back home we carried on chitchatting about this and that, but neither of us touched the two contentious topics: our past and our original reason for meeting. If I say our goodbye was incredibly awkward, I am not exaggerating. But what is the appropriate way to say goodbye to a guy you agreed to meet to explore kinky sex, but who turned out to be a heartbreaker from the past who wants to make amends and be your friend?

He walked me to my door and I had to stop myself from giggling because it felt very much like some cheesy Hollywood romcom movie. But then, of course, there was no kiss or declaration of feelings. Instead we just stared at each other, waiting for the other person to say something. Eventually Smutty decided he'd had enough and started to scrape the door, meowing pitifully to make it clear that he was very displeased with me coming back so late again.

"Give me your phone," Ben had demanded, and his tone made me somehow putty in his hand because I handed my mobile over and unlocked it for him. Not sure what voodoo that was.

"Now you have my number and I have yours," he smiled. "Anything you need or if you want to chat more, or join me and Coop for lunch, call me. Or text me." He gave me a cheeky wink. He bloody winked! Does he not know that this is catnip for women around the world ? I just stood there gawping as he strolled back to his car, but then Smutty went absolutely mental inside and I finally tore myself away.

So, for the last seven days I've looked at his number more often than at gifs of my favourite actor and I'm not even sure why. It's not that I've forgiven him, but his words just keep making more and more sense the longer I think about them. Spending time on the dating app has convinced me that I want to give this a try. Another daydream of a dark and handsome guy gently squeezing my throat whispering, "Now, darling," made me come so hard yesterday that I squirted! Smutty came running into the bedroom in a panic because I had also screamed out loud and he probably thought someone was attacking me. Not that he was necessarily concerned about me, but he probably was worried that he'd lose his personal slave.

But as much as I want this, so far everyone that has contacted me on the app has been rather strange. Aside from Ben of course. I have only had odd messages.

Michael

> **Does your cat like to watch.**

I mean, fuck off.

And then there was Roger, who told me he wants to pleasure me with a brush. The first brush I saw was the round barrel with metal bristles on my vanity table, which I think would land me in A&E. No, NO!

Oh, and the Lord was back:

Wilfred

> **Lord Anal Pain is not pleased with you. Beg for forgiveness.**

And... blocked.

I know there must be plenty of genuine people on this app but just like with mainstream dating apps, I seem to attract only the weirdos. All I keep hearing are stories of people who meet their significant other online, and I can't even find a casual pleasure dom who doesn't want to defile me with a brush.

Which brings me back to Ben. He was right, we have seen each other naked... a lot. And from memory Ben was a mighty fine sight, even the deflated baby mole dangling between his legs. That memory makes me snort because he hated it when I referred to his penis as the baby mole. Mole as in the blind animal living underground, not a birth mark. And just to make it clear, I didn't refer to it as baby because it was small. Nope, he had no problem in that department... had, has? I guess the size wouldn't change over years. No, I once came across the image of newborn moles on the internet and, what can I say, they have a certain genital look.

So here I am, doing the most insane thing I have done in years. Probably more insane than when I decided to book a full AFF course (that's Accelerated Free Fall course) before even doing a test skydive. I thought I could take up skydiving as a new career. Luckily, the skydiving school insisted I do a test tandem jump first. I ended up clinging to the inside of the plane calling the instructor a flying arsehole, which I had to apologise for once the plane landed safely. Needless to say that the school and I both agreed that I wasn't suited to it.

Okay, Amelia, you can do this. Do it... do it... DO IT! Just rip the metaphorical plaster off.

I hit the call button. The phone rings once, twice.

"Hello, Amelia." It's so unfair that his deep and smooth voice still makes me weak in the knees.

"Hi," I reply nervously and I sound a bit squeaky. "Are you busy?" I crawl on top of my bed and cross my legs. Smutty jumps and curls up in my lap as if he can feel that I need his calming influence. In reality he probably just has an itch he wants me to scratch. My fingers start stroking between his ears and he purrs.

"No, I just got back from a run."

"Still a fitness freak?" I giggle but I'm just stating the bleeding obvious because it's clear he works out from looking at him.

"Running helps me relax," he replies and he now sounds muffled. "Hang on."

Smutty rubs his head against my hand, the little attention whore. Obediently, I give him a cuddle.

"Sorry, I'm back," Ben's voice makes me jump. "You just caught me as I was getting changed." Uh, the baby mole was out in the wild. I bite my lip so I don't giggle.

"Amelia?"

"Sorry, yes, I'm here." I blush, even if he can't see me.

"So, not that I'm not glad to hear from you, but after the dinner I thought—"

"Does your offer still stand?" I blurt out.

This wasn't quite like ripping off a plaster, it was more like ripping off a super sticky tape from your nipple.

"Just to be clear, you mean—"

"To help me figure out this... stuff." I breathe heavily and suddenly realise I sound like I'm aroused rather than just incredibly nervous.

"Are you sure?" His voice is calm and unfazed.

"Yup, I mean, if you want. You were right when you said we already kind of know each other. Have seen each other's bits. And I know you won't hurt me. Physically." I breathe out.

"Amelia—," he replies frustrated before adding with some alarm in his voice, "wait, are you suggesting you want me to show you what it means to be with a pleasure dom, not just answer your questions?"

10

Curiosity

Amelia

*O*H SHIT. MAYBE HE was just joking at dinner. I feel my face heat up again.

"I... well, I mean... If you want."

"What about you hating me?"

"I told you I don't feel hate. I feel nothing." Contrary to what I've said, my heart starts pounding faster, and a flurry of butterflies dance in my stomach. But that's just because I'm anxious he might say no, I'm sure. I genuinely want to try this submissive thing now that I've set my mind on it. And once I've made up my mind there's no turning back. If he were to say no now I'd be deflated.

"Okay. Not sure feeling nothing is much better, but I think I get what you mean." His voice is quieter than a minute ago.

"If you don't want to, Ben, I would underst—"

"No, that's not it. Sure, okay, fine." *Uh, thanks, don't sound quite so excited, why don't you?*

"As long as you don't call my dick a baby mole," he adds and I grin. He remembered. And he's joking. *That's a good sign, right?*

"Scouts honour."

"You were in the cubs."

"Fine, cubs honour." I relax back against the headboard as a sense of relief engulfs me. Smutty decides to give up trying to attract my attention and struts out of my bedroom with one last disapproving look back. I scramble off the bed to close the door. "So, how do we do that?" I nervously nibble on my bottom lip as the door clicks into the lock, shutting out Smutty and stopping him from judging me.

"Well, tell me what you'd like to try."

"I don't know. Not hitting."

"Spanking. Hitting is something different, but I get it, no spanking. Any other nos? Or anything you are particular interested in? Actually, let me ask you this: what fantasies made you want to give this a try?"

"I... I don't know." The bed sags under me as I crawl back onto the mattress.

"Amelia, you need to be open with me if you want to try this. I need to understand what you're hoping for and what you don't want. There's no right or wrong answers. We'll only do what you want, what excites you. Your taste may change over time. Something that sounds exciting now, might not be quite so appealing once you have tried it, or things you don't want now might get interesting. All of this is fine but you need to talk with me about it."

"No spanking," I object again.

"I know. I got that," he replies patiently.

"The thought of not being in charge excites me. The idea of not having to be the strong person, the person in control. I like the idea of someone taking care of me. Of telling me what to do." As I say the words out loud a warm feeling spreads through me. Yes, this is definitely what I want. "Please tell me if that is just weird, or not what you do, or—"

"Amelia as I said, there's no right or wrong. But your idea of letting someone else control your pleasure fits exactly with what I do and what I enjoy as a... PD," he chuckles as he uses my abbreviation for pleasure dom.

"It's weird, but if you told me what to do in life I would probably tell you to go and fuck yourself because I'd hate it. I hate when people tell me what to do like I'm an idiot or a small child. But when it comes to sex, the idea..."

"Gets you horny?" he finishes the sentence for me.

"Yes," I agree, blushing deeply again.

"No, it's not weird, Amelia. But do you understand this will require trust? Can you trust me?"

His question hangs heavy in the room. *Can I?*

"I get that and yes, I think I can trust you with this."

"Okay, so now tell me your fantasies." My mind is racing. There are so many things, and I'm clearer on what I don't want.

"No spanking."

"Amelia, I promise you, no spanking," he assures me again.

"I like the idea of doing stuff in public but I don't want to be caught. I don't want to be embarrassed or humiliated." There is no response. "And, and I have used a butt plug sometimes whe—" I stop talking. I'm mortified that I just admitted that.

"With other men?" There's an edge to his voice.

"No! On my own... It feels good." I bury my face in my hands.

"Okay, got it. Just toys?" he asks with no judgment in his voice. The fact that he doesn't laugh at me calms me down a little and I lean back again.

"Well, I haven't tried going full in the bum, so to speak. So for now just toys back there, I think."

"Darling, anything you want."

"Was that public thing too much?"

"No." He doesn't elaborate on why he stayed quiet. "What about being tied up?"

"I'm not sure. I definitely don't like the idea of handcuffs or ropes or anything like that. It feels quite brutal to me personally. No judgment," I add in panic in case he's into that.

"None taken. It's not for everyone and requires an extra level of trust."

"Oh, okay."

"Amelia, I don't say this lightly, but you can trust me."

"I'm new to all this," I admit sheepishly. "I mean, I've read books and watched movies, but never actually done anything other than vanilla sex."

"That's perfectly fine," he insists. "Everyone starts somewhere. And exploring your desires is all about taking things at your own pace."

His words are comforting and make me feel less anxious. Maybe this won't be as scary as I thought.

"But enough talking," he says suddenly, interrupting my thoughts. "I want you to do something for me."

My heart skips a beat at his commanding tone. *What does he want me to do?*

"I want you to touch yourself," he says simply.

I freeze for a moment, not sure I heard him correctly.

"You want me to do what?" I stammer.

"Touch yourself," he repeats firmly. "I want you to masturbate while we talk."

I feel the heat rising to my cheeks as I process his words. This is definitely not what I was expecting.

"I... um... I don't know if I can do that," I mumble, suddenly feeling shy and self-conscious.

"Amelia, it's okay," he says gently. "I'm not trying to pressure you into anything. But exploring your sexuality is an important part of this. And what better way to start than with some self-pleasure?"

His words make sense, but it's still a bit overwhelming. I've never had phone sex before.

"Take your time to think about it," he adds. "There's no rush. We can continue talking and see where things go."

I take a deep breath and consider his offer. This is an opportunity for me to step out of my comfort zone and embrace my desires. I wanted this and he's giving me the first chance to explore my fantasies.

"Okay," I finally say, surprised at my own boldness. "I'll give it a try."

A smile tugs at the corners of my lips as I hear the satisfaction in his voice.

"Good girl," he says approvingly. "Now put your phone on speaker and tell me, are you wearing any underwear?"

He's straight to the point causing a thrill of excitement to course through my veins.

"Yes, sir," I reply breathlessly. I don't know where that came from. He hadn't asked me to call him anything different, but in this moment I just felt like it. It was my way of showing him I am at his command.

"I want you to take them off," he instructs.

My fingers tremble as I reach down and pull my knickers off, dropping them on the bed beside me.

"Now lie back and close your eyes," he continues. "Let your hand slide over your breasts and tweak one of your nipples."

I shudder a little and not because of the cool air in the room. For a moment I panic, but then I remember it is Ben on the other end of the phone and I relax.

"Move your fingers lower, Amelia." I love hearing him say my name. "Imagine that it's my hand between your thighs, teasing and pleasuring you."

A soft moan escapes my lips at his words as I do as he says, letting the image fill my mind.

"Now touch yourself," he commands gently. "Start by running your fingers along your folds, feeling how wet and ready you are for me."

I let out a shuddering breath, my fingertips gliding over my slick heat.

"That's it," he murmurs. "These are my fingers stroking your pussy, circling your clit, driving you wild with desire."

His words are like delicious torment, intensifying the sensations lighting up my body.

"Are you enjoying this, Amelia?" he asks.

"Yes, sir," I gasp.

"Darling," he purrs. "Now focus on your clit. Rub it in slow circles, increasing the pressure with each stroke."

I moan loudly as I follow his instructions, pleasure building within me with every touch.

"I can imagine how beautiful you look right now," he says huskily. "Lost in pleasure, all because of me."

His words send a jolt of desire straight to my core, pushing me closer to the edge.

"Let me hear you, Amelia," he demands.

I part my lips and a tiny moan escapes me.

"Mmh, tell me what you're thinking."

"I wish it was your hand, sir," I whisper.

"It soon will be, darling," he exhales.

Just at that moment, Smutty decides to scratch on the door to be let in. I grab the pillow next to me and throw it against the door with my free hand shouting "Fuck off!" *That bloody cat! I was so close.*

"Sorry?" a confused Ben asks.

"Oh, not you, it was Smutty... my cat on the door."

I hear Ben chuckle.

"Ignore your cat, Amelia, and focus on your pussy. Rub your clit for me," he demands. "But don't come yet."

I whimper at the thought of being denied an orgasm but do as he says, rubbing my swollen nub in slow circles and trying not to let myself get too carried away. I've never had much control over my release and I'm not sure if I'll be able to hold out much longer.

"That's it, darling. Now slip a finger inside yourself."

I moan as I push one finger between my wet folds, moving in and out slowly whilst I continue to rub my clit with my other hand.

"Faster," Ben commands. "Fuck yourself faster."

I obey, picking up the pace as I pump two fingers into my pussy. My breathing is laboured and every so often a groan escapes me.

"That's it," Ben says approvingly. "Just like that. You're doing so well for me."

I moan at his praise, feeling myself getting closer and closer to the edge with every stroke of my fingers.

"Are you ready to come?" Ben asks.

"Yes, sir," I gasp.

"Stop touching yourself."

I freeze at his command, whimpering in frustration as I deny myself the orgasm that is just within reach.

"Tell me how wet you are."

"I think there is a wet stain on my bed." *Lovely.* Total dirty talk failure.

"Hmm, all for me," Ben doesn't seem to be put off by my words. "Now touch your clit again. But don't come yet."

I groan at his words but do as he says, resuming the slow circles on my clit that had been driving me wild just moments before.

"That's it," Ben says encouragingly. "You can do it. Just a little longer now."

I whisper his name as the pleasure builds once again, this time even more intense than before. I can feel myself teetering on the edge of an orgasm, so close that it hurts, but I force myself to hold back, not wanting to disappoint Ben by coming without his permission.

"Are you close?" he asks.

"Yes," I gasp.

"Yes, what?" *Oh fuck*, looks like I'm not the only one who likes the *sir* game.

"Yes, Sir," I moan.

"Good girl." I shudder at his praise for me. "Now pinch your nipples for me."

I whimper at his command, reaching up with one hand to tug at my sensitive nub while I continue to rub my clit with the other.

"That's it," Ben says. "You're doing so well for me. Just a little longer now."

The pleasure is almost unbearable, radiating out from my clit and spreading through my entire body like wildfire. I'm ready to explode and I know that I won't be able to hold back much longer.

"Let go, Amelia," he whispers. "Give in to the pleasure and come for me."

I cry out his name as ecstasy crashes over me like a tidal wave, sweeping away all thoughts and worries.

As I come down from my high, panting and sated, I can hear the satisfaction in Ben's voice.

"Well done, Amelia," he says warmly. "You did beautifully."

"Thank you," I say softly. "I mean it, Ben. I didn't think I could do this without dying of embarrassment."

"Thank you for trusting me," he says casually but I can't help thinking there is much more to his words.

11

Try Losing One

Ben

THIS IS THE FIFTH time I've read this email and I still have no clue what it's about. Ever since my call with Amelia at the weekend I can't think about anything else. My brain has gone into overdrive mulling over the many reasons why this is a bad idea, and counter-arguments of why this is a brilliant idea. I'm torn, but one thing I know for sure: hearing her come apart took everything in me not to head over to her cottage. *Focus, focus!*

I scan the report from our Swiss subsidiary again when the door opens.

"Morning!" Coop grins at me as he strolls into my office.

"Morning. Weren't you supposed to be in Canada for another week or so?" I press enter to send the email.

"Too cold. I tell you, there is cold and there is Canadian cold. We basically stayed in bed the whole time. And so, we thought if we cut the holiday short we could jet off on a beach vacation in a few weeks," he grins.

"Well, two weeks in bed with the woman you love doesn't sound like hardship. So don't expect any sympathy from me."

"That part was great." He grins.

"And? Are you going to tell me what she said?" I raise an eyebrow. He knows exactly what I'm asking.

"She said yes, of course," his grin gets bigger, if that is even possible. I rise from my chair and pull him into a man hug.

"Congratulations!" I hate to admit it, but I'm a little choked up . Coop has wanted this for so long.

"Thanks, mate. Which brings me to our little discussion from before the trip." He takes a seat as I drop back into my chair.

"The general manager."

"Yes. Ben, I really think we need this—"

"I agree," I interrupt him.

"You agree?"

"Yes. Is that not what you wanted me to say?" I smirk.

"I did. But that was too easy. What happened?" He gives me a suspicious look.

"Nothing. I just realised that I don't have the same fire in me anymore. Taking it easier sounds good." I try to keep my expression neutral even if Amelia's face immediately comes to my mind.

Coop looks at me carefully before pulling his phone from his pocket.

"Fine. Don't tell me. I'll email the agency now and you better not change your mind." He points at me. "Anything happen whilst I was gone?"

"I had a few conversations with Neil regarding the contract. He's still playing hard to get, but we all know he needs that deal as much as we do." Henderson Steel Works is a company in the Midlands, and we have been talking with them for a few months about a new construction project we have coming up.

Coop mumbles his agreement about the deal as he types away on his phone.

"Oh, guess what, I ran into Amelia." Silence. I had to tell him at some point and, in all honesty I'm dying to talk to him about it.

"Amelia?" He locks eyes with me. "Your Amelia?"

"Yup," I reply casually like it is not a big deal even if it is a big fucking deal.

"Where did you meet her?"

"She, well..." His stare makes me feel like I'm on trial. "We matched on the dating app I use."

"The BDSM app?" There is surprise in his eyes when I nod. "I didn't think Amelia was into that."

"Neither did I," I shrug.

"And?"

"We met up for dinner and—"

"Hang on, is she the cat lady?" Coop rises from his chair.

"Yes."

"Ben! Fuck. I saw the look on your face when you texted her. You're falling for her again."

"No! That's not what this is." I protest but somehow it doesn't really feel true to me either.

"How is it, then?" he challenges me.

"It... she asked me to show her what it means to be with a pleasure dom."

"You're kidding me?" Coop looks stunned.

"No—"

"Tell me you said no!"

"Coop—"

"Ben! For fuck's sake. What are you doing?"

"I'll tell you if you let me finish a bloody sentence," I raise my voice and square up to him.

Coop inhales deeply before taking a seat.

As I recap what happened, of course leaving out the phone sex, he keeps shaking his head.

"I think this is bonkers, Ben," he sighs when I finish my story.

"I know. But I couldn't say no to her. If I can help her with this I will."

"And what happens if she walks away again at the end?"

"I... I'll let her go of course." But I can hear the uncertainty in my voice.

"Don't hurt her, Ben!"

"I'm not the same man, Coop. I'd give her anything she asks for. I think that makes me much more likely to get hurt." As I say it out loud I know it's true. There is no point in fighting it. I need to admit the truth to myself: when she stood in front of me in the restaurant my old feelings came roaring back to me. I would have given anything to hold her in my arms.

"Fucking hell. This is madness. I'm worried for you, and for her."

"I know," I reply. We stare at each other. Before either one of us can say anything else Gladys sticks her head into the office to get Coop who is late for a meeting.

After he leaves, my fingers casually glide over my phone. As the screen springs alive I click on the dating app. Amelia's profile is the first one on my list. I take a couple of screenshots of it then press the little red cross.

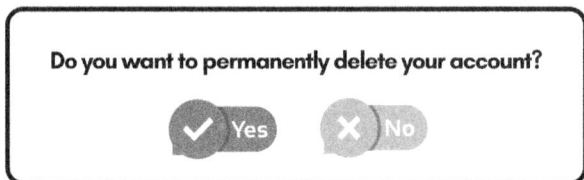

Do you want to permanently delete your account?

✓ Yes   ✕ No

I hit yes and follow the final steps. That's it. As long as Amelia is around there isn't going to be anyone else.

12

Bleeding Love

Amelia

SAMIRA TAPS HER WATCH. That's my ten-minute warning to get my shit together because we are heading out for lunch. A new Brazilian street food stand has opened around the corner and we want to give it a try.

I open the attachment to an email from the finance team. It's an invoice for my approval. I quickly scan over the page. The logo doesn't look familiar. When I get to the description of services I stop. *Analysis of the security situation in Balochistan.* I didn't order that.

"That, that—" I blow out hard because I can't find a word that is appropriate for the open plan office. My outburst draws Samira's attention.

"Everything okay?"

"Richard," I hiss. Samira rolls her eyes but doesn't ask for details. She knows that whatever he's done I am most likely in the right.

I can't believe he just went ahead and ordered an analysis. I told him no. *But not with me my friend, not with me.* I hit the reply button on the email.

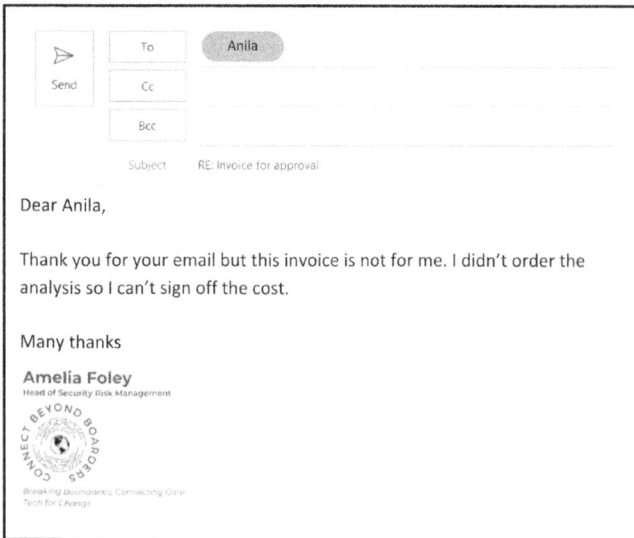

Dear Anila,

Thank you for your email but this invoice is not for me. I didn't order the analysis so I can't sign off the cost.

Many thanks

Amelia Foley
Head of Security Risk Management

Breaking Boundaries, Connecting Care
Tech for Change

I grin to myself and grab my handbag. Now I deserve a nice lunch.

"**O**H, FUCK THIS IS amazing," I moan taking another bite of my sandwich.

"I see dark times ahead for our bank accounts," Samira grins. I can only nod as I devour another piece of the chicken delight.

"So, are you ever going to tell me about your date with the pleasure dom?" So far I have managed to dodge her questions not only because I still blush when I think of the phone call, but also because I don't want to relive Ben and my past. As luck has had it, she was on annual leave until now which offered me some reprieve. I should have known that I wouldn't get away with it forever.

"Not much to say," I shrug. *Liar!*

"Well, so far all I know from your very cryptic message is that it's someone you know from your youth."

"We dated in our twenties." I mumble before stuffing my mouth with more bread. Samira stops chewing and stares at me.

"And he didn't tell you before you met?" Her eyes narrow.

"No, he... well, our relationship didn't end well and he wanted an opportunity to talk to me. He knew I wouldn't turn up if he'd told me who he was."

"And? Oh my god, don't make me drag every crumb of information out of you."

"And... we chatted. We talked about what happened. He apologised. And that was it. Kind of."

"Kind of? There's more?"

"No—"

"Amelia," a familiar voice interrupts me. Miranda waves from across the street before looking left and right and quickly crossing. *Oh, great!*

"Hey," I greet her with a kiss on the cheek. "Miranda, you remember Samira?"

"Oh yes, hi," she smiles at Samira before taking a seat. "I'm sorry to interrupt your lunch. I was about to call you tonight and now I might as well tell you here." She fishes a chip from my paper plate. "Stress eating," she explains before stuffing it in her mouth. "So, Ben is back."

Two things happen at once at Miranda's words: my cheeks heat up and Samira stiffens in her seat.

"She had a date with him," Samira suddenly blurts out, making both me and Miranda snap our heads towards her. Miranda's eyes widen in surprise, whilst I shoot Samira a disapproving look

"You... you had a date with Ben?" Miranda looks stunned.

"It's not what it sounds like. He contacted me via the app Bea set up and—"

"But you hate him! I came to give you a heads up that Sim-Sim has invited him to the wedding and you've been dating him all along? Amelia! Can I remind you how much he hurt you?"

I guess that's fair. *She's right, of course she is right.* However, a persistent little voice in the depths of my mind insists that this time, things might be different.

"He's changed." I mumble causing both Samira and Miranda to laugh. *Since when are they on the same side?*

"Amelia! You're forty-one years old. When will you grow up? People don't change."

"Now that's a lot of bullshit. As you just pointed out yourself, people grow up*." Ha, that's a point for me.* "Besides, we're not dating. We went for dinner, nothing else." *Liar*! Immediately my cheeks burn.

Miranda gives me a suspicious look. "So, I don't need to worry that you'll cause a scene at the wedding?"

"I don't cause scenes." I put the last word in air quotes. I am anything but a scene maker.

"What I meant is you acting like a lunatic because you're trying to avoid him." Oh, okay, that does sound like me.

"No. Ben and I spoke. We're good."

"Okay. Excellent," Miranda grins and nibbles on another of my chips. "I have a favour to ask, though. My cousin Peter has no date. Can I put him on the table with you so he has someone to talk to?" Now it's my turn to narrow my eyes.

"Is that a set up?"

"No!" she replies way too quickly and her tone makes me suspicious.

"It is a set up," Samira mouths to me and grins.

"Please?" Miranda pleads.

"Fine." I really have to learn to say no.

"Wait, why was Ben on that kink app?" Miranda sits up and leans forward.

"He's a pleasure dom," Samira smirks.

"I don't know what that is," Miranda replies.

"He puts a woman's pleasure first." Samira explains.

"Sounds like a pickup line to me."

"That's what I said," Samira exclaims and holds out a hand for a high five. I'm not sure how much I like them becoming friends and ganging up on me.

"Okay, I need to hear more," Miranda stares at me.

"Sorry, can't do, we have to go back to work." I've never been more eager to get back to work.

"Fine. But I really want to know the whole story. I'll call you and we meet up for coffee." Miranda picks up her handbag from where she placed it on the floor.

"Okay." What else can I say?

I PULL MY phone from my jacket pocket as the train rolls through the outskirts of London. I have another message from Ben.

Ben

> How has your day been?

He has texted me a few times and I've ignored all of them. Every time I have convinced myself that there is nothing wrong with what we are doing, doubt sets in again.

That phone call was something else. It's crazy to think that I let him talk me into it but in that moment, it felt... right. It's hard to articulate, but it didn't feel odd or weird; instead I felt safe. It was like something I'd been looking for. I can't describe the thrill it gave me to call Ben "sir".

I have wondered if it was Ben or if it was just the submissive thing that made it feel so right for me. Truth is that I can't imagine doing this with some stranger, some random person who I didn't know. The fact that Ben was familiar definitely helped.

But then where is this going? I'm an analytical person. Whatever happens in my life, my brain will immediately create possible scenarios on where this could lead and all the issues that could come up. But with this situation I can't imagine what could happen next because I have zero experience with it. It's not a normal, everyday situation and I can't see an end point. And that scares me. It makes me feel out of control. I can handle normal situations. You meet a guy on a date and there are two outcomes, you fall for him or not. You start a relationship or you don't. But Ben and I know we won't start a relationship. How can we? So, what, we are friends with kinky benefits? And what if he meets someone and has to cut me off? What if he wants kinky stuff I don't want?

But what if it does work out this time. What if we kind of rekindle the feelings for each other again? *Oh, here is my inner optimist again, painting rosy scenario of a fairy tale ending.*

Argh, I'm so confused. I close my messaging app again. Until I have some clarity in my head there's no point in texting him.

Now I just need to ignore that feeling in the pit of my stomach. That longing to hear his voice.

13

Like a Virgin

Ben

I STRAIGHTEN MY CUFFS as I weave my way through
the wedding crowd. I haven't seen or spoken to Amelia
since our phone sex session and I'm feeling on edge. She
has ghosted my messages and I can't help but worry that
it was too much too quick for her and so she's pushed me
from her life again. The call was not what I had expected,
but it had me rock hard at the end and I had to wank off
with her whispered "sir" still in my ears.

On my second sweep of the banquet hall I finally spot
her at a table tucked away in the far corner. I'm not sure
why she's not sitting with the rest of our friends up front

near the top table and a frown forms on my face. A bloke is sitting next to her, the spotlight from the ceiling reflecting of his bald head. He is persistently leaning in for an intimate chat, their faces almost brushing against each other. Without a second thought my legs guide me towards her, but just before I reach the table she utters something, rises from her chair, and strides away. It's only when she catches sight of me that she halts in her tracks, a flush of embarrassment instantly colouring her cheeks.

I grin and let my eyes travel over her body. She's wearing a flowery dress with a frilly skirt and a low-cut top. Too low cut for my liking, given the stares that guy is giving her.

"Amelia," I greet her and gently cup her elbow to drag her further away from the table.

"Hi, Ben," she replies with an edge of hostility in her voice. *Why is she angry with me again?*

"You've been avoiding me." I lock eyes with her. I need to see the truth; I need to see if I pushed her too far.

"I... Ben, I think I made a mistake." As her gaze drops, a surge of panic floods through me. My heart races... I'm about to lose her, I can feel it.

"Do you really think that?" With a finger under her chin I lift her face so she has to look at me. "Amelia, tell me honestly, did you enjoy our call?"

"I—"

"Don't lie." My voice is firm.

"Sure, but—"

I lean forward, sliding my arms around her waist, and whisper in her ear, "Did you enjoy it when I told you to touch your clit?" I can feel her squirm.

"Yes," she breathes.

"Did calling me sir turn you on?"

"Yes."

"And did you have an amazing orgasm?"

"Yes." She gently holds onto my jacket as if she needs something to steady her.

"Then how can this be wrong?"

"It's not what normal people do."

"Who are these normal people? We have no clue what goes on behind closed bedroom doors, believe me! Forget others. Nobody knows about this. Think about yourself. If you want this, I'm here for you." I take a step back and she almost tumbles forward when she can no longer lean against me.

"Why are you sitting all the way in the back?" I ask, casually changing the topic, and nod to the table. The eyes of her admirer are boring into me. Oh, he's definitely interested in her and not pleased to see me whisper in her ear. I gently stroke my hand over her back and leave it just above her delicious bum to stake my claim. Childish, I know, but he needs to know she's mine.

"Miranda paired me up with her cousin, Peter." She turns towards him and quickly turns back when she finds his eyes on us.

"Are you interested in him?" *That didn't sound jealous at all, knobhead.*

"No! He just told me what his favourite microwave dinner is because he can't cook and then asked me if I'm a good cook. I mean, I know I'm not the most exciting person, but even I want more from life than a bit of nooky over a microwave meal." Her comment makes me snort.

"I think you missed the point where he wants you to cook for him," I chuckle.

"Ben!" She slaps me playfully, but there is a twinkle in her eyes.

"And I think you proved last week that you are anything but boring, darling," I whisper in her ear.

"Ben." This time my name sounds like a moan.

"Dance with me," I demand.

"Why should I?" Amelia crosses her arms. She tries to fight me but her eyes betray her. I know she wants this.

"The way I see it, you have two options. Dance with me or get dragged back to the cousin by Miranda. It's your call, darling."

I put my hands on her shoulder and turn her so she can see the bride approaching with Peter.

"Oh shit," Amelia whispers. "Fine, you win, one dance!"

We'll see. I take her hand and drag her past a surprised-looking Miranda and a scowling Peter. When I pull Amelia to me my cock thickens. She feels so good and so perfect. I close the distance between us and start to sway with her in my arms. My fingers slide over her curves and when I cup an arse cheek a little moan escapes her. Since our call I haven't been able to think of anything other than letting my fingers go where hers had been.

"Do you like that, darling?" She doesn't say anything so I squeeze a little harder. "Answer me."

"Yes," she sighs.

"Good girl." There's that shudder again. "Tell me how wet you are."

"Ben! I am not—" I stop her with a rough kiss. *Oh fuck.* It meant to stop her talking, but I suddenly realise that this is our first kiss in twenty years and it lights a fire in me that I thought had died forever. The taste of her, the warmth of her tongue as I slide into her mouth, the gentle pull when she sucks on my bottom lip. It is familiar but also new and for a moment I forget why I kissed her.

"Don't lie to me," I groan when I eventually break away. I can see the conflict on her face. I know she is worried that people will judge her. But she is equally excited by the prospect of testing out where this will lead her.

"I don't know," she finally says and lowers her eyes to the floor. A beautiful pink is spreading across her cheeks. I grab her hand and drag her from the dance floor.

"Where are we going?" she asks in protest as I lead her down a corridor.

"In here." I push open a small door to a room that I assume the hotel uses for meetings. It's dark, but the streetlamps lining the driveway to the venue cast a little light into the room.

I press Amelia against the wood panelling and kiss her hard. My tongue dips into her mouth and she moans. *Yes, it feels that good.*

"Spread your legs," I demand.

"What?"

"You heard me, darling. Spread. Your. Legs. Now." She hesitates for a second, but when I raise an eyebrow and throw her a challenging look, she slowly parts her thighs.

I kneel down in front of her and slide my hands up underneath her dress until they find her knickers. My fingers hook into the material on the left and the right and drag them downwards until they pool at her feet. I stand up and lock eyes with her.

"Let's see, shall we?" I pull the hem of the bottom part of her dress up until her pussy is exposed. Slowly, one of my fingers glides over her cunt and is immediately coated in her juices. "So wet," I groan, and my fingers draw lazy circles around her clit before two of them enter her pussy.

Amelia moans loudly and grabs my shoulders.

"Does this feel how you imagined last week?"

"Better," she groans.

"Darling, put your hands against the wall."

"Ben, I—" She stops talking and moans again when a third finger enters her.

"I said, put your hands against the wall. You have one second or I'll stop." A shiver races through her body but she is finally my good girl and presses the palms of her hands against the panelling on either side of her.

"Yes, sir," she whispers. *Fuck, that made my dick twitch.*

"Now, listen to me." My fingers pump lazily in and out of her wet pussy. "You are not to come until I tell you to. Do you understand?"

Amelia whimpers but eventually replies, "Yes, sir."

"This is my body to control," I growl, and my free hand tightens carefully around her throat. "Mine."

"Yours, sir," she confirms. Her eyes are closed, and her mouth is open. Her breathing is getting faster. I keep moving my fingers in and out of her wetness and add a little extra pleasure by circling her clit with my thumb.

"Fuck," Amelia hisses and her hand grabs my bicep. I withdraw my hand and take a step back. Amelia opens her eyes and looks at me bewildered.

"No, Amelia. I told you I would stop if you moved your hands."

"Please, sir, I'm sorry, sir." It is amazing how quickly she slips into her submissive role.

"Let me help you, darling."

I grab her wrists and place her hands against the wood.

"Leave them right there," I whisper and rub my nose up and down her neck, breathing in her delicate smell.

"Please, I need more, sir."

"Because you asked so nicely," I chuckle and lift her skirt again, kneeling down in front of her and pressing my lips just above her mound.

"Ohhh," Amelia moans, "What if someone comes, Ben?"

"Nobody will find us here." To be honest, I'm not one hundred percent sure that's true but the chances are slim considering that the staff are busy with the wedding. "Come whenever, Amelia, give me your pleasure." I command before sucking her clit into my mouth. This is not the right place to edge her. If we get discovered she'll end this here and now and that is not something I want to risk. I slide two fingers into her cunt and the wetness and warmth make me groan against her swollen nub.

There is a gasp from Amelia and she is tilting her body forward to press her clit firmly into my mouth. I suck harder and with her pussy strangling my fingers I can feel how close she is. I gently scrape my teeth over the hardened bud and simultaneously press my digits on her g-spot and that's all it takes for her to moan out loud as the orgasm rushes through her. I can't help but grin as I pull her knickers back up her legs.

"What do you say, darling," I whisper in her ear.

"Thank you, sir!" she whispers. The minute her words leave her lips she surprises me by dropping to her knees in front of me.

"Amelia, you don't have to—" I try to stop her as she reaches for my zip. I remember that she was never particular keen on sucking my cock.

"I want to, Ben——sir," she replies with pleading eyes as she pulls my dick from my trousers. She looks so innocent kneeling there on the hardwood floor, her blonde hair cascading around her shoulders as she focuses on my cock with single-minded determination. Her lips wrap tightly around me, her tongue swirling and flicking in all the right places. *Holy shit, where did she learn that?* I can't remember her doing this before.

I watch her intently as she works me over. Her bright blue eyes look up at me from beneath thick lashes, full of desire. She knows exactly what she's doing to me and she loves it.

"Fuck," I groan, my fingers tangling in her hair as I try to keep some control and not push her down on my cock. "Darling, that feels amazing," I encourage her.

She hums in response, sending vibrations down my shaft that make my knees weak. She closes one hand around the base of my dick and moves it in tandem with her mouth.

I can feel myself getting closer to the edge with every passing second. My hips start to thrust involuntarily causing my dick to slide deeper down her throat making her gag. I pull back to allow her to breathe.

Amelia looks up at me with a grin. "Please, sir."

Did she just beg for me to come in her mouth? I lean forward, bracing myself against the wood panelling. I don't know what has come over her but she seems to have found a new side to herself in her submission.

Before I can protest or beg for more she takes me back into her mouth , going even deeper than before. The sensation is overwhelming——wet heat surrounding me on all sides——and I have to fight to keep from coming right then and there.

She keeps up the relentless pace, her tongue and lips working magic on my hard cock. I'm lost in a haze of pleasure, unable to think or speak or do anything other than feel.

Finally, I can't hold back any longer. I let out a strangled moan as I come hard in her mouth, my whole body trembling with release. She swallows every drop, never breaking eye contact .

When she's finished she pulls back and wipes her mouth with the back of her hand. Heat spreads to her cheeks as if she realises what she's just done. I gently grab her upper arms and help her up.

"That was incredible, darling."

"Thank you," she whispers.

"You know you didn't have to do that."

"I know, but... I felt I wanted to."

"You never did in the past," I say as I tuck my dick back into my trousers. I can't help bringing up our history yet again.

"You weren't my PD then," she sniffles and a tear rolls down her blushed cheek.

"Fuck, did I hurt you?" I ask and cup her cheek, wiping the tear away with my thumb. There is that panic again.

"No!" She shakes her head and gives me a grin through her tears. "I don't think I've ever felt more like myself than just now. I can't describe it, Ben, it's weird but it's true."

I pull her into my arms and place a soft kiss on her forehead. *Fuck, I shouldn't have agreed to this.* I can say for certain that I won't be able to keep my heart out of this game and I am not convinced she can either. But I'm in too deep already. I don't want to break it off. I need to see where this is going and deal with the consequences as and when they rear their ugly heads.

14

Holding Out for a Hero

Amelia

S MUTTY STRETCHES AND YAWNS lazily. The smell of his cat breath hits me and I wrinkle my nose.

"Time to cut back on the tuna," I tell him. All he hears is the word tuna and he's on high alert. I just shake my head and he, somehow, seems to get that it's not time for his favourite treat.

My phone vibrates.

Ben

Are you hiding from me again? ;-)

Yes, okay, I'm avoiding him again. After our little make out session at the wedding I snuck out of the hotel as soon as it was socially acceptable and without a goodbye to Ben. I was confused, that's the only excuse I have. I had no clue how to deal with this situation and as the chicken shit that I am, I only saw one solution: to hide. He must be getting tired of my hot and cold treatment soon.

Whenever he leads me down the PD road I willingly follow him and, oh my word, what he delivers in orgasms and pleasure is mind-blowing. But then we come back to reality and I wonder if I've gone insane. That's the man who broke my heart years ago. But the more time I spend with him, the less I dwell on the past and the more I see the good in him. The little optimist in me screams that maybe he really has changed before past Amelia pipes up reminding me of the pain he caused.

Argh, I'm a bloody mess and I hate myself for it.

I ignore the message and instead shuffle to the kitchen. It is bloody freezing in here. I'm already wearing pyjamas, socks, a hoody, and a bathrobe. The minute I get off the sofa Smutty sneaks under my blanket. Poor little kitty is also cold.

Tap, tap; the controls on the central heating are on twenty-two degrees so it should be roasty toasty in here. One touch of my radiator tells a different story though.

It's ice cold. *Fuck. That's the last thing I need.* I grab my phone from my sofa ignoring another message from Ben and instead turn on my torch app. The light of it is just enough to illuminate the small room in the kitchen that houses my boiler. It is unusually cold inside it, given that the heating was supposed to have been on all evening.

Shit! One look at the boiler dials shows me that it has zero pressure and is clearly not working.

"Fuck!!" I shout, making Smutty jump. He's left the warmth of the blanket out of nosiness and followed me. My little black shadow.

"Sorry!" I call out after him as I scroll through my contacts and find the number of my landlady, Harriet. I walk into the kitchen and close the door. All I need is for Smutty to meow at the wrong time and I'm in deep shit because my rental agreement does not allow a cat. I did ask Harriet once (when Smutty was already living with me), but she was adamant: no cats. I couldn't really kick Smutty out so I've been hiding him ever since. Luckily he's a housecat and doesn't venture outside, so it's not like my neighbours see him walk in and out.

"Hello?" Harriet's croaky voice sounds through the phone.

"Hi, it's Amelia from Taylor's Close."

"Amelia, everything okay?" I never call her. I'm an easy tenant, which is why I was doubly annoyed when she wouldn't allow me a cat.

"Yes, no... I think the boiler is playing up. All the radiators are cold and it looks like it doesn't have any pressure," I explain whilst turning on my hot water tap to see if there's been a miracle and it's only the heating that's impacted

"Oh, I'm sorry, Amelia." I mean, aside from the cat thing, she is actually a very nice person. "I'll call the plumber now and will make sure we come over tomorrow," she assures me.

"Oh, don't worry, I can work from home, no need for you to head over, I can let him in." *Please don't hear the panic in my voice, please!*

"Nonsense. I haven't done a property check in a while in any case. And this way I can deal with him directly, which should hopefully speed up the repairs."

Fuuuuuucccckkkk.

"Oh, okay. Sure. What time do you think you'll be here?"

"I'll let you know once I've spoken to the plumber but I'll aim for some time before noon."

I thank her and hang up in a state of hysteria. *Smutty! What the fuck am I going to do with him?* I scroll through my phone. Miranda is on honeymoon and Samira is allergic to cats. I press the call button next to Bea's number.

The phone rings and rings whilst I walk back to the living room. Smutty has returned to the warmth of the blanket and gives me a dismayed look when I lift him so I can sit down and pull it over us.

The phone rings out and goes to Bea's voicemail. I leave her a short message telling her about the boiler and ask her if she can take Smutty for a few days before hanging up and trying again. She may just have been on the toilet or something. The phone rings a few times before she finally answers.

"Amelia, is everything okay? You never call." She's right, we are more a text message group than a call group.

"Bea, can you take Smutty for a few days, please?" I plead.

"What? Why?"

"My boiler is broken and the landlady is coming over with the plumber in the morning. Please, Bea, you know I can't have him here. She'll go ballistic if she finds any trace of him." Lucky for me, he doesn't scratch the furniture or carpet so aside from his litter box, food, toys, and scratch post, there isn't really anything around to give away that he lives here.

"Sorry, hun," she sighs dramatically, "but I'm very busy at the moment. I can't take on looking after a cat."

"He is very easy." I mean, he is. Feed him, cuddle him and he's happy.

"Sorry, Amelia. Maybe it's time to give him to a shelter." *Fuck you*, is what I want to shout at her.

"I can't do that." There is silence on the line, and Bea is clearly not offering help or any other solutions. "Anyhow, I have to go," I end the call. *Thanks for nothing. Why am I friends with her again?*

The first tears trickle over my cheeks. I can't give him away. I love him. He's curled up in a small black ball in my lap, purring away as I gently stroke his soft fur.

I sniffle and open the search engine on my phone. I google catteries in the area. Okay, let's throw money at the problem.

"Don't you worry. I'll get you somewhere safe." Smutty ignores me, the ungrateful little twerp.

Half an hour later I want to throw my phone on the wall. As it is already after seven in the evening most places are closed. I eventually found one that had an out of office hours number and a lovely person called Bridget answered. She totally understood my problem and told me all about the Purr Inn which sounded a bit crazy. A bloody tablet in each cat's room so you can talk to your feline companion at any time. Luxury furniture, a TV and gourmet food. Smutty would have never wanted to come back if I put him there. But it's just outside Little Hadlow so I could visit him if he has to stay longer. Then she told me the price and I almost choked. One hundred pounds a night. I can't afford that. Maybe for a night but I've been here before. It's unlikely the plumber can fix the boiler tomorrow, especially if has to order parts, and then it's the weekend. We could be talking four if not five nights. That's half of what I pay rent for my house for a whole month.

I thank Bridget and end the call. *What the fuck am I going to do?* More tears and a little sob escape me before I pull Smutty closer. He graciously lets me cuddle him for a bit before gently biting my hand.

My gaze falls on my phone again. Another message from Bea apologising and Ben's message that I haven't read yet.

Ben

> Please at least let me know you are okay.

I take a deep breath. *I can't, can I?* One look at Smutty and I know I have to at least try. *Fuck it.* Before I can change my mind, I type a message.

Me

> Are you at home at the moment?

Immediately the little three bubbles appear telling me that he is typing.

Ben

> Yes. Why?

Me

> Okay, what's your address?

Ben

> Are you going to answer any of my questions?

Me

> Want me to come over or not?

Okay, maybe I am leading him on a bit here but I'm desperate. He's my only option. I try to recall if he is a cat or dog person but I can't remember and frankly, I don't care.

A few seconds later my phone lights up with another message. Ben's address. He lives at the other end of the village near his sister; so too far for me to schlepp all of Smutty's stuff on foot.

Me

> Okay. Stay there. I'll be with you in 30 mins or so.

I don't wait for his reply but go into full on mission mode. I put on yoga pants and a half decent jumper before packing up every little toy Smutty has, all of his food, his litter box, spare litter, and the fluffy cat bed he never sleeps in but might want to in a strange house. I dig out the cat carrier and with a ton of treats finally coax Smutty into it. He doesn't look pleased but doesn't cause a racket either.

The taxi I booked straight after I texted Ben is on time, but it takes me five minutes to convince the driver to take me and Smutty despite his no pet policy. It takes us another ten minutes to try to fit the scratch pole and all of Smutty's possessions into the boot before we make the short drive to Ben's.

I'm surprised when the taxi driver stops outside a nice but reasonably sized house. I expected Ben to live in one of these outrageously oversized villas that are on almost every corner of the village now that Little Hadlow has become a commuter dream for the London bankers. But instead, Ben's looks fairly humble and not like a house that shouts "I'm rolling in so much money I can waste tons on sending a dick shaped rocket into space."

The driver grumbles under his breath when I ask him to help me unload but eventually we have everything placed outside Ben's front door. I wait until the taxi disappears around the corner——I want to give Ben as little excuse as possible to send me away——and then ring the doorbell.

"Darling," he smiles as he opens the door. Oh, he definitely thought this was another PD session. His face falls when he sees me there in my messy hang-around-the-house clothes, surrounded by boxes and bags and a cat carrier in my hand.

"Amelia? What the f—"

"Be good and give me a hand," I say pretending there is nothing amiss here before pushing past him with Smutty.

Oh wow, this is nice. His house is decorated expensively, but tasteful and homely. I can see dark furniture and shelves with books in the first room on the left. That's where I place Smutty's carrier, so he is out of the way, before turning back to Ben. I was expecting more of a fight, but he's picked up the scratch post and placed it inside the door to the left. He's now carrying the box of the cat food and most of the bags into his house.

"Care to explain?" He tries again when our eyes meet.

"Let's just get this all in first," I say and shoo him down the corridor leading to the back of the house. I place the cat litter tray next to the scratch post before grabbing the last of the bags and closing the door.

"Now?" Ben makes me jump as he appears behind me.

"Sure." I push the bags into his hand and wave him off again.

My chest expands as I take a deep breath of relief. Smutty is in. He is safe. That's all I care about even if I basically performed a hostile takeover of Ben's house. I know I sound a bit nuts but I also know Ben will let me get away with it.

Smutty's pink nose appears through the grid on the door as I lift his carrier. He sniffs the air of his new surroundings as we head in the direction that Ben disappeared. At the end of the corridor I find a living room and a kitchen. Ben is in the kitchen staring at all the bags.

"Ben, I need your help," I start, and his eyes land on me before zoning in on the cat carrier.

"No! No, Amelia. I don't like cats!" he exclaims with big eyes.

"Oh, come on! Smutty wouldn't hurt a fly," I coo and open the cat carrier door. My beautiful black furball jumps out and immediately attacks one of the tassels of the rug on the floor. I laugh nervously when Ben raises an eyebrow.

I try to swat Smutty off the tassel but he takes that as a sign for a little rumble and attacks my hand with his ears pressed tightly against his head. He carefully sinks his teeth into my palm whilst clamping on tightly with his paws. He would never hurt me but even I can see that this doesn't look good.

"Clearly, tame like a lion," Ben says, crossing his arms in front of his chest.

15

Smelly Cat

Ben

THIS ISN'T GOING TO happen. I have never and will never be a cat person. Amelia is standing in front of me with messy hair, nervously pulling on her ratty T-shirt. Her eyes are full of fear. And I feel a small crack in my armour.

"Ben, please." She takes a step closer. "My landlady has to make some repairs to my boiler tomorrow morning, and I can't find anywhere else for Smutty to stay. She doesn't know that I have him because she won't allow cats. Please." Her voice breaks and a tiny tear runs down her cheek. Amelia is not someone who will fake cry to get what she wants. Come to think of it, Amelia is also not a person to ask for help. If she's here begging me to take her cat it must be serious and mean a lot to her.

"Come here." I hold out my arms and she takes tentative steps before finally allowing herself to sink into my embrace. It feels so natural, so right.

"Smutty is my whole world. I can't let my landlady know that I have him, she'll make me give him up. I can't lose him," she cries softly into my chest. *Ah fuck, how can I say no to that?*

"Fine."

"Fine?" She lifts her head and gives me a big grin. "Did you hear that, Smutty? You can stay with Ben!" The only response we get is some awful retching before the cat spits a tiny furball onto my kitchen floor. Amelia's cheeks turn pink and she rushes to grab a kitchen towel from the counter.

"He doesn't do that often. If he got it out now he'll be good for a few weeks," she mumbles apologetically as she mops up the vomit.

"Sure." I wipe my face with my hands. This is so not how I'd imagined this evening would go. "Do you want some dinner?" I ask her.

In the hope that's what she was coming over for I defrosted some pasta sauce.

"No, can't, sorry. I have to go home and make sure there's nothing left to give Smutty away. Right, he gets dry food throughout the day and wet food in the evening. All the food is in the box. You should put the litter box somewhere he can easily get to and place him in it at least three times tonight even if he doesn't need to go, so he remembers where it is. There are tons of toys but mainly he just sleeps," she rattles off instructions whilst retreating towards the door. Smutty and I follow her, not ready for her to leave.

"Bye, Smutty." She picks up the furball, cuddles him and presses her lips to his head. He gives a little meow before she places him on the floor again.

"Thank you, Ben. I'll text you all the instructions." She places her soft lips on my cheek and it takes everything for me not to pull her close for a proper kiss. She's given me blue balls the whole week, ignoring my messages again after that evening we had and clearly there is no relief in sight.

She slides out of the door before I can reply, leaving me and the cat alone in the corridor. He sits on the floor next to me and stares at the closed door.

"Welcome to my house, I guess." I stuff my hands in my jeans' pockets and grin at him. He just gives me a look of discontent before turning his nose up and walking away from me like I don't exist. *Fuck my life.*

OKAY, I SWEAR THIS furball hates me already and he's only been in the house for an hour. I put the cat litter tray in the utility room. The first time it took ten minutes for me to catch him so I could show him where his fucking toilet is. But he's not stupid; the second time he saw me coming and had me chase him through the house for twenty minutes before I finally cornered him. In return, he gave my hand a swipe and I now wear three red scratches as a badge of honour.

But we're not done. He and I are eyeing each other again. It's like he knows that I need to put him into his litter box at least one more time. But before I can make a move, my phone rings.

"Hello?"

"Hey, are you busy?" Coop asks.

"I'm locked in a battle at the moment. What do you need?"

"What battle?" he asks ignoring my question.

"Long story. Actually, do you have a clue about cats?"

"Cats?"

"Yes, how do you catch one?"

Coop chuckles before I hear him repeat my question to who I assume is his soon-to-be wife.

"Lizzie says use food." *Fuck, of course!* I head to the kitchen to try to find some treats.

"So, what do you need, Coop?" I say and peek into all the bags on the floor. Eventually I find tins of cat food in a box.

"The recruitment agency confirmed our meeting tomorrow to discuss the general manager role," he sounds determined.

I grab the box of dry food and shake it which seems to work like magic because I barely finished rattling it when the black furball shoots into the kitchen like a lightning bolt.

"Ah, gotcha'" I chuckle.

"Sorry?" Coop asks from the other end of the line.

"Not you. Yes, I'm up for a meeting with an agency. The important thing for me is that we keep control over the bigger picture decisions."

"Shit, Ben, me too. We worked too hard, but I need some more time to enjoy life. I need this," he sighs.

"I get it, Coop. And I agree."

"I won't ask where this change of heart is coming from," he replies.

"I didn't have a change of heart, I never said no," I argue, but we both know I'm full of shit. When he originally told me about the plan I wasn't ready to give it all up.

"Okay let's talk tomorrow. But, Ben, I'll say it again, whatever this with you and Amelia is, make sure you know what you're doing. Neither of you can cope with more heartache."

"I told you that's not what this is about." *If I fight it, it isn't true, right?*

"Still. I'll see you tomorrow."

I put my phone on the kitchen counter. My eyes drop to Smutty, who is still sitting in front of me staring longingly at the food.

"Alright then, one more look at the toilet and you can have some food, Furball," I say and walk towards the laundry room. I put a few pieces of the dry food on the floor. Smutty looks at it and then back at me and back at the food. Only when I step aside and out of reach of the litter box, he finally strolls in and licks the food from the floor.

My phone pings to alert me to a message.

Amelia

Right, here are the instructions.

She attached an image. It's a photo of a handwritten note.

Congratulations on being entrusted with the care of my precious feline companion! Below are some essential instructions to ensure you and Smutty have a harmonious time together:

Mealtime Madness:
Feed Smutty dry food throughout the day. Put half a cup in his bowl in the morning and don't give him more. He will beg and cry but he knows he can't have more. In the evening you can give him one of the small tins of gourmet food. The tins are in the box.

The Great Litter Conundrum:
The litter box is a sacred space. Scoop it daily and place each "gift" in the outside bin. Refer to the litter box as "Poo Palace."

Enrichment Extravaganza:
Engage in at least 30 minutes of playtime. Smutty enjoys mouse football and loves watching videos of birds.

Cuddling Catastrophe:
Smutty appreciates cuddles but only on his terms. He will let you know when it's time for a snuggle session. Don't resist the purr therapy.

Window Watcher Protocol:
Keep the curtains open so Smutty can monitor the neighbourhood.

Cat-versation Etiquette:
Engage in meaningful conversations with Smutty. He has strong opinions about the state of the world, particularly about the scarcity of gourmet treats.

Bedtime Rituals:
Read a bedtime story to Smutty. He prefers tales involving heroic cats saving the world.

"Hey, Furball, that's not going to happen, I'll tell you now." I stare at the cat. He stares back before climbing into his litter box and squeezing out a little "gift" telling me exactly what he thinks of me.

Me

> You better be fucking kidding 'cause otherwise you can pick him up right this minute.

Amelia

> The last bit was a joke.

> I can come by tomorrow and take care of most things. What time will you be home?

I sigh and eye the cat again, who is now scratching cat litter on top of his turd. *Lovely.*

Me

> I'm out all day but my housekeeper will be in until five. If you pop by at any time before five he can give you a key so you can come over whenever you want to check on him.

> You haven't told me how long he'll be my guest.

It better only be a few days!

I don't really need her to come over because Gustavo can just feed that cat, but I have a feeling the offer to visit is not just to lessen the burden on me but also because she wants to see Smutty. And I will take any chance I get to spend some time with her. That's my reward for housing the furball.

Amelia

> Oh, are you sure? I don't want to bother you, but I can do the whole list so you just need to give him the food in the morning.

> It's only for a couple of days. Four at most.

I head to the living room and am about to drop into my recliner chair when I notice that the cat apparently agrees that this is the best seat in the house. He's lying curled up on the leather recliner and couldn't care less that I'd like to sit there.

"Cat, move it," I command. He briefly opens one of his eyes, glances at me and then snuggles back down and ignores me. *Well, fuck you too.* I'm about to lift him from the chair when my eyes fall on the scratches on the back of my hand. Maybe this one time, I'll just let it pass. *The sofa is comfy too, right?*

Me

No, it's fine. Come whenever.

Amelia

Thank you again Ben. I mean it! I know I railroaded you into this but THANK YOU!

Me

You're welcome!

"Furball, am I making a mistake?" I ask. Coop's words echo in my brain. *Make sure you know what you do.* I know exactly what I'm doing but that doesn't mean it's a good idea. In fact I'm worried it might be the worst idea I've ever had.

16

Great Balls Of Fire

Ben

THE CURTAIN PULLS BACK and the nice nurse from earlier tells me that she is just getting the last of the paperwork done. I should be able to leave in ten minutes or so. I nod and grab my jacket from the gurney next to me. I try not to move too much because the pain is still strong.

My phone is in my left pocket and I wiggle it out before opening my message app.

Me

> Just so you know, I'm in hospital because of your cat.

I'm about to put my phone back when it vibrates with an incoming message.

Amelia

> Oh my god, is Smutty okay?

I roll my eyes. *Of course her first thought was for the black furball.*

Me

> I'm in hospital, not the damn cat.

Amelia

> What happened?

Me

> He used my testicles as a trampoline when jumping onto my lap. The doctor has diagnosed testicular trauma.

I won't tell her that we were playing with one of his mouse toy thingies when things got out of hand. The cat has turned me into a right sap.

Amelia

> Oh, he likes you if he jumps on your lap.

> Me
>
> Did you not hear me?? Testicular. Trauma.

There's a no reply. I grin because it's not really that bad. The doctor confirmed that it's just a mild case and the pain should subside fairly quickly, but Amelia doesn't know that and I think I deserve some pity.

> Amelia
>
> Okay, I googled it. So basically you have a bruised bollock.

> Me
>
> That's right.

> Amelia
>
> Did they have to untwist it?

> Me
>
> No.

> Amelia
>
> Was it dislocated?

> Me
>
> No.

> Amelia
>
> Did they have to remove it?

Me

No

That little minx is taking the mickey!

Amelia

Ben, did they give you an ice pack and tell you to rest for a few days?

Me

Yes!

Amelia

Fucking hell. I would say grow a pair but apparently you have a pair, just some very weak ones.

The cheek.

Me

I'll have you know they're not weak.

I can't believe I am defending my bollocks.

Amelia

I'm not sure how to reply to that.

Me

Well, for one you can say you'll pick up your cat.

I frown. I don't really mean it. I've actually got used to having the furball around. It's been a week since she has dropped him off with me——the plumber is taking his good old fucking time——and we've somehow got into a routine. *Oh fuck, total sap.*

Amelia

> I can't! The plumber is still waiting for parts and probably won't be able to repair the boiler before next week.

> Sorry.

Me

> It's freezing.

Amelia

> Oookay?!

I could kick myself for not thinking about that before. We've had a cold spell kick in two days ago, bringing arctic winds. She must be freezing in her house with no heating or hot water. She made sure her bloody cat had a safe and warm space to sleep whilst she stayed in her ice-cold cottage.

I press the call button on my phone and wait for her to answer.

"Yes?" Amelia answers dragging the word out sarcastically.

"Amelia, pack your bags, you're moving in with me."

"I beg your pardon?" She sounds like a posh lady from a period drama.

"You. Will. Stay. With. Us." *Wait, I just called me and the furball "us"?*

"No, I won't." And there she is, the person who hates nothing more than accepting help, unless it is for her bloody cat apparently.

"Yes, you will."

"It's fine. My landlady gave me an electric heater, and I can boil water in the kettle and I take a shower at work—"

"Amelia! For once, can you accept some help? I have two spare bedrooms. You can pick whichever you prefer. And you can be with the cat."

"Smutty," she corrects me. She went mental on the weekend when she came over to say hi to him and caught me calling him Furball. We had a minor argument, mainly because she was so cute when she was angry that I kept poking her by calling him anything but Smutty. To be honest, it is a bit of a ridiculous name.

"Exactly," I reply and grin to myself. *I'm an arsehole.* "Pack a bag."

"No."

"I'm not asking, Amelia. I'll be there in an hour to pick you up and if you're not done, I'll pack for you and you'll only have knickers to wear all week," I threaten jokingly but my mind flashes to her damp knickers on the floor at the wedding and I have to hold back a groan.

"Is there any point fighting you on this?" She huffs in frustration.

"No." I end the call. I'm in for a serious case of blue balls again and not because of the bruises her cat caused.

"I TOLD YOU I don't need to move into your house," Amelia greets me when I get to hers.

"You come with me." I won't take no for an answer. She is wearing a hoody, a jacket and what looks like three pairs of socks. The weather forecast is predicting that this cold spell will continue for at least another three days and there is no way I'll leave her here. I'm still furious with myself for not thinking about moving her in sooner.

"It's not that cold," she argues and tries to cross her arms in front of her chest. They barely meet, though, because of the many layers she is wearing.

"You look like Shackleton on the way to the South Pole," I joke and gently shift her out of the way so I can step into her cottage. "Are you packed?"

"No," she says defiantly.

"Fine," I climb the stairs to the first floor where I assume her bedroom is.

"What are you doing?" she shouts from behind me.

"Packing," I reply just as I get to the landing on the upper floor. The door to the left is open and I can see a bed covered with two duvets. A tiny electric heater provides a minimal amount of warmth. "Fuck, darling, why didn't you tell me?"

"It's not that bad." But there isn't much conviction in words. She sounds defeated and sad. I just shake my head and pull a drawer open.

"Not that one!" she shouts making me jump back. My eyes land on the contents of the drawer.

"That's a lot of vibrators." My voice is strangled as I try not to laugh. It's not the vibrators I find funny; the idea that she isn't the wallflower she appears to be is hot and not new to me given that she made out with me at the wedding. It's just that this whole situation feels like a French farce.

Amelia pushes the drawer closed with her cheeks burning bright red.

"Kill me, kill me now," she mumbles.

"Hey." I gently cup her chin and make her look at me. "There is nothing to be embarrassed about! Nothing."

She studies me but doesn't reply.

"Now, please pack a bag, Amelia. I can't leave you here. They're saying minus five tonight. I need to know you're safe," I say with my voice fading to a whisper when I admit more than I should. I lean my forehead against hers and draw in her scent.

"Okay," she finally replies and takes a step back. "I have some more of Smutty's food in the kitchen. You must almost be running out. Can you grab it please?" she tries to shoo me out of the bedroom, probably so she can pack without me snooping.

"No need, I bought more yesterday," I shrug. "I have to make a few calls for work though. The trip to the hospital has put me behind schedule."

"Oh, shit. Sorry, I forgot about your dangly bits. I'm sorry that my tiny cat hurt your—" She points at my crotch and smirks.

"Your sincere concern for them is heart-warming." I can't help myself from grinning.

"What do you want me to do? Blow on them and tell them it'll all be better soon?" The minute she realises what she just said, her cheeks turn pink again. "I mean—" she stutters.

"I leave you to the packing. You have ten minutes," is all I reply. As much as I enjoy our banter, I'm freezing my arse off in here and I'm pretty sure Furball is waiting for his dinner.

WHEN WE FINALLY MAKE it back to my house the cat nearly has a fit because he wants his gourmet dinner. Amelia, of course, obliged him before spending another thirty minutes cuddling and playing with him. Now she is having a hot bath whilst I prepare dinner. It's all starting to feel a bit domestic and I like it, which I'm not sure is a good thing.

"Hey," Amelia draws my attention. She's leaning against the kitchen door with her wet hair in a towel.

"Feeling warmer?"

"So much. I love having a bath," she sighs.

"Well, you can have as many baths as you want whilst you're here," I tell her, carrying two plates to the table.

"Oh, you didn't need to make dinner. I could have ordered us a takeaway," she argues before taking a seat.

"Worried I'll poison you?"

"No." She carefully sniffs the plate of tortellini in tomato sauce.

"Hey, I'm a decent chef, I'd like you to know," I mock protest as we laugh.

Amelia takes a spoonful and moans, "Wow, that's amazing."

"I know," I wink and we settle into a comfortable silence whilst eating. When we're nearly finished, I tell her about mine and Coop's plan to hire a general manager and my initial hesitation.

"So, what made you change your mind on hiring one?" Amelia asks, scraping the last of her sauce.

I shrug. "Coop was right. We need to start enjoying our life a bit. We've been working nonstop since we left university."

"Okay, but why did you hesitate initially?" Amelia probes. I try to think about how to answer that.

"Coop has Lizzie. They want to travel and explore the world. I have an empty house. It feels sometimes lonely." Amelia swallows hard. "Forget what I said. I think I'm entering a midlife crisis. But luckily I have Fi, my niece and nephews, and I want to at least spend more time with them." *And I want to spend time with you.* Fear of scaring her off stops me from saying it out loud. And yet, it is the one thing I want to say more than anything else.

17

If You Don't Love Yourself

Amelia

I STARE AT THE empty plate in front of me. It would be easy to fall back to light-hearted conversation but something stops me. I need to say this. I need to. *Be brave, Amelia. For once, open up to someone. You are safe with him.*

"I tell you what being lonely means," my voice barely above a whisper. "Lying at home in your bed, watching TikToks and a simple video of a couple hugging is enough to make you cry."

I have never told anyone this and I'm not sure why I'm telling him now, but I feel the urge to say what I've kept to myself for so long out loud . Ben's eyes are on me but I can't meet them. I don't want to see the pity in them that I'm sure is there.

"To get some comfort," I continue, "I sometimes pull a heavy pillow against my back and pretend it's someone lying behind me whilst I cry my eyes out." I sniffle. "That makes me sound insane, doesn't it?"

"No, it doesn't." His deep, smooth voice contains no mockery so I look at him. His eyes are on me but there is no pity on his face. Sadness, maybe, but no pity.

"It is. I'll tell you something else insane." I slide my chair back a little and hug my legs to my chest. "My number one wish is to find love of course," I confess. "To live with someone who truly loves me, someone who, when I walk into the room, has eyes only for me. Someone who wants to know what my day was like and who knows when I need him to just be there for me." I stare at the table. "But do you want to know what my second wish is?" I ask, hesitating.

"Sure," Ben replies gently as if scared he'll spook me.

"I want someone to take me into a room and tell me over and over what all my flaws are," I reveal. "That I'm fat, I'm ugly, I'm boring, I'm uptight, I'm whatever else is wrong with me. I want them to hurt me so much that it kills the pesky optimism I have, this belief that everything will be alright in the end. Because it never is. I want to be hurt so much that I'm just numb and no longer have any hope."

Ben looks at me, concern etched across his face. "You don't mean that," he says.

"I do, seriously" I insist. "I could just live my life without the constant wish for more, for something better and someone else. I might finally be happy with the life I have. As far as I'm concerned, optimism is the greatest evil. If you're a pessimist forever expecting the worst you can only come out on top. If something works out despite your doubts, you'll feel like a winner. If it doesn't, well, you still win because you never expected it to go smoothly. Now, if you're an optimist, sure, things might work out, but they rarely unfold the way you imagined they would. And when you don't get what you dreamed up, the crash is epic. I hate being an optimist but I can't flick the switch. It's ingrained in me and I can't alter it. I have tried! To curb my enthusiasm, to take things one day at a time, but optimistic thoughts sneak in and set me up for a fall, especially when it comes to relationships."

I swipe my finger over the rim of the plate to wipe up some sauce before licking it off my finger.

"I'm forty-one years old, and in all those years nobody has ever loved me. I've never been someone's first priority."

Ben opens his mouth to speak, but I cut him off. "No, I know that the issue is me. I'm not blaming anyone."

He looks puzzled. "How can you say that?"

"Think about it," I urge him. "What's the common denominator in all of these disappointments? Me. Clearly, it's me."

Ben searches for words, but he doesn't seem to know what to say.

"You probably wonder why I don't change. That would be the easiest thing, right? That's what people have been telling me all my life. Lose weight, lower your expectations. Don't tell men about your work, they don't like strong women. Nobody wants to hear about that trip to Guatemala. Why are you so boring and don't drink? You're so cold. Oh god, can you stop joking and take things seriously," I rant and tears sting behind my eyes. Ben just studies me.

"I've tried. Fuck, have I tried but every time I change something that someone has criticised me for, they find something else wrong with me. I've lost weight, changed my personality, but it made no difference. I'm tired. I want to be me. I want to be accepted for being me." I slam my hands against my chest. "The thing is that I don't mind all the things people judge me for, I even like some of them. I see myself as adventurous with my travels and I'm proud of it. I love being successful in my job. I think I can be funny, sometimes. I don't drink by choice and I'm not sure why that makes me boring. But why am I the only one who likes those things?"

Ben draws in air as if he wants to say something but I stop him again, "I know, I know. I also heard more than once 'You shouldn't care what others think.' Usually from the same people who kindly advised me how to shape my personality differently. And, in theory, it's not bad advice. Fuck them and just be me. But what if every single person that ever meant something to you wants you to be different? What if you want nothing more than to have one person in your life who accepts you for who you are?" Angrily I wipe my tears away. "I've never had someone look at me in love, like there's nobody else but me for them."

Ben interjects, "I did, Amelia."

"No, you didn't," I counter bitterly.

"Yes, I did," he insists. "Do you think maybe you just don't see when someone looks at you like that?"

"Maybe. See, that's another thing wrong with me. I'm in this catch-22, Ben. I have been told so often that things are wrong with me that it's incredibly difficult to believe when someone tells you something nice. The thing is," I continue, "if someone tells you something hurtful, the only goal they can have is to hurt you. It's transparent. If someone tells you something nice they could have many goals. They want something, they lie because they don't want to hurt you, or they're trying to manipulate you."

Ben considers my words for a moment. "How about they mean it?"

"There is that," I admit. "The problem I have is that I'm shit at reading which one it is."

"Maybe everyone is bad at that," Ben suggests. "Because everyone hopes that the other person means it."

I shrug. "Maybe, but in my experience, they never do. So now I just mistrust people from the get-go, which is then another thing: pushing people away, which in turn makes me think everything is wrong with me and——" I look up at him and there is a storm raging in his eyes. "What if I die before anyone ever honestly tells me that they love me?"

I need to stop. I sound insane and I can only imagine what Ben must be thinking. One more thing to add to the list – neurotic weirdo.

Suddenly I'm aware of the silence in the room. My question hangs unanswered in the air. I lock eyes with him but It's difficult to read what he's thinking.

"Sorry, I'm not sure what came over me. I've never told anyone that," I whisper. I grab our plates and take them to the sink. His chair scrapes on the floor as he gets up.

"Thank you for telling me." He turns me and pulls me into his arms. For a second, I think of fighting him but then I let him draw me in. His warmth engulfs me and the simple contact makes me shake with tears. I can't stop crying so I bury my face in his chest.

"Have you ever considered talking to a therapist?" he asks carefully, his hand gently stroking my back.

"For another person to tell me what is wrong with me?"

"That's not how therapy works, darling. But you have been hurt, hurt too much and it's driven you down a rabbit hole. A professional can help you to deal with the hurt."

"I don't know."

"I went when my mum died," he says like it's not a big deal.

"Did it help?"

"Yeah," he snorts, "it made me realise again what a twat I was when I was younger and how much I hurt you, and it helped me learn to deal with it... Amelia, I don't think we should continue with the PD thing."

I lift my head from his chest, "Why? Oh god, I've put you off with this soppy story. I'm sorry, B—"

"Don't! You have nothing to be sorry about. I've hurt you badly in the past. I'm the reason you are feeling the way you feel. How can we continue with this? Frankly, I don't understand why you don't hate me more." I can see pain on his face.

"You hurt me back then and you might be one of the reasons that I think I'm not good enough the way I am. But this all started way earlier in my childhood, and it wasn't just you. Ben, you're different now. When I'm with you I don't think about the young guy from years ago. And I'm no longer the same woman. I'm a messed-up cat lady with an extensive collection of vibrators," I joke and sniff at the same time. "But I've never felt more like myself, more accepted for who I am, than when you pinned me against that wall and told me to spread my legs. For the first time in a long time that wasn't me doing something I thought someone was expecting me to do. I was doing it for me, because I wanted it. Please don't take that away from me."

Ben cups my face and places another kiss on my forehead.

"I'll go and ice my bollocks now," he tries to give me a grin. It's a half grin, but at least he didn't say no. I can't let him take this away from me.

Ben

I GRAB AN ICE pack from my freezer and head to my bedroom without another word to Amelia. I need to get out of the kitchen. When the door falls into the lock behind me I stare at the walls.

Fuck, fuck, fuck, fuck. I want to scream out loud but I don't want to distress Amelia even more. I almost can't fight the need to throw something, punch something, but this is my bedroom. The best I can do is throw a pillow, and I don't think this will have the same effect.

Hearing her talk ripped my heart into a thousand pieces. I can't believe that I caused her so much pain. I have done this to her. The best thing would be for me to admit that I don't deserve her and walk away, but that would just hurt her again. No, I need to give her a chance to take whatever she needs from me.

I really am the biggest arsehole on the planet.

18

Time After Time

Amelia

S MUTTY'S TAIL WHACKS ME in the face. He isn't the easiest bedfellow. I press the button on top of the alarm clock and the numbers light up. It's just after one a.m., which means I have been tossing and turning for three hours now and I'm nowhere near sleepy. The look on Ben's face scared me. He looked ready to walk away from all of this and I wasn't lying when I said that I haven't ever felt myself as much as I did in the moments when I submitted to him.

The memory of his lips on mine and his fingers and... It makes my clit tingle and I press my legs together to subdue the need. I still feel raw from the conversation earlier and what I need now is to feel good. I need him.

"Smutty, stay here," I whisper and slide from the bed. My little black shadow couldn't care less and continues to snooze. When I reach my bedroom door I hesitate for a moment. This is insane. But it's what I want. I want this so much. I catch sight of myself in the mirror. I'm wearing an oversized T-shirt that hangs off me like a sack. Not really sexy.

I tiptoe to the chest of drawers and dig around. Aha! I knew I had packed that soft black nighty. As I take my shirt off and slip the nighty on, my eyes fall on the plain blue knickers I'm wearing.

I slide them off as well and dig in the drawer again until I find the green lacy ones. I don't tend to wear them because they're uncomfortable and a bit too tight, but, with some luck I won't be wearing them for long.

I slide them up one leg before stepping into them with the other foot. Somehow, I underestimate how much smaller they are then my normal ones. My toe gets tangled in the lace and I hobble on one leg trying to free the other. In my attempt, I lose balance and crash against the small chest of drawers, slamming it against the wall behind it. A bottle of hand cream falls over with a loud bang. I freeze, knickers halfway up both legs, and listen out to see if the noise has woken Ben. But there is just silence in the house. I give it a few seconds whilst my heart hammers like crazy, but when the everything remains silent I pull the knickers all the way up and look at myself in the mirror.

Okay, sure, yes, kind of cute, but still me. I rub my upper arm where I crashed into the chest of drawers. I'm sure I'm going to have a bruise in the morning.

"Wish me luck, Smutty," I whisper before slipping through the open door into the dark corridor. When I get to Ben's bedroom door I listen again for any noises but there are none. Of course, that perfect bastard isn't snoring.

I gently press the handle down and push the door open. His curtains are ajar and a glow from the street light is falling through the window. I take a few steps closer to the bed.

What am I doing? I should just leave. But I can't tear my eyes away from Ben's sleeping form. His strong, muscular body is sprawled out beneath the covers and soft breaths escape his parted lips.

I take another hesitant step forward, the floor creaking under my weight. Ben stirs slightly, his brow furrowing as he senses my presence. Panic sets in, and I turn to retreat to the safety of my own room.

"Amelia?" His voice is groggy with sleep, but it stops me in my tracks.

I turn slowly to face him, unable to meet his gaze. "I... uh... I was looking for Smutty," I stammer. *Come on! That's the best you could think of?*

His eyes narrow slightly as he studies me. "Smutty? In here?" He glances around the room before settling his gaze on me.

"Yup, you remember, black little furball," I joke nervously.

"You mean like the one sitting behind you in the corridor," Ben grins. I whip my head around and see the little traitor looking at us expectantly to see what all the kerfuffle is about.

"Oh. I'm sorry, my mistake," I mumble, avoiding his gaze. "I'll just go."

Before I can make another move towards the door, Ben is on his feet and crossing the room towards me. My heart races at his proximity, and all thoughts of leaving evaporate.

He stands before me, close enough that I can feel the warmth radiating from his body. "Amelia," he says softly, lifting a hand to brush a strand of hair behind my ear. "You don't have to go. If you want this, I'm all yours, but this is your call ."

His touch sends shivers down my spine and I look up at him through lowered lashes. The air crackles with tension as we stand there in silence. I walk past him, gently closing the door to the corridor, a silent promise that I'm not going anywhere. My heart races with anticipation; *yes, I'm choosing this*. When I turn, Ben stands before me, his gaze filled with longing and desire.

Slowly, oh so slowly, his hand slides down from my hair to the curve of my neck. His fingers stroke lightly over my skin, leaving a trail of heat in their wake.

"Please, Ben," is all I say.

I close my eyes at his touch, a soft sigh escaping my lips. His gaze darkens with desire as he watches my reaction and I can feel the heat pooling between my thighs.

Taking my words as the invitation they were meant to be, Ben's other hand grasps the hem of my nighty. He tugs it upwards, exposing the bare skin of my stomach inch by agonising inch.

I raise my arms obediently as he pulls the shirt over my head and tosses it aside. Standing before him in nothing but the pair of too-tight knickers, I feel exposed and vulnerable under his intense scrutiny.

His eyes roam over my body, taking in every curve and dip. "You're fucking beautiful," he growls, his voice thick with desire. "And you're all mine."

"You don't need to say that," I whisper.

"I'm not just saying it." He grabs my hand and places it on his chest, right above this heart. "Feel that?" His heart is racing and I take comfort from it. "Or this?" he adds and places my hand on his erection. "That's all you Amelia."

I can't stop a smile forming on my lips at his words and I feel ready to surrender to him completely. This is what I've wanted, what I've craved ever since he returned to my life. We are travelling on a dangerous path but in the moment I couldn't care less about possible future heartache.

Ben's hands are on me again, tracing a trail down from my collarbone to the swell of my breasts. He cups them in his hands, kneading them gently as he thumbs over my hardened nipples.

A moan escapes me and he smirks as he continues to explore my body with his hands and mouth. He leaves hot kisses along the valley between my breasts before moving lower to nuzzle against the fabric of my knickers.

"Spread your legs for me," he commands, his voice rough with need.

I do as he says without hesitation, parting my legs slightly to give him better access. He tugs on my knickers and they slide to the floor.

"Step," he makes me lift my legs so he can remove them.

I stand before him completely naked, my body on display for his pleasure. I've never felt so vulnerable, so exposed, and yet it's the most exhilarating feeling in the world.

He kneels before me, his eyes locked with mine as he traces a path up the inside of my thigh with his fingers.

"Tell me what you want," he says in a low and commanding tone.

"I want... I want you to touch me again," I whisper, my voice barely audible.

A predatory smile tugs at the corners of his lips as he leans forward to press a kiss against the apex of my thighs. "With pleasure," he murmurs against my skin.

His tongue darts out to trace a slow circle around my clit, and I gasp at the sensation. He teases me mercilessly with his tongue, flicking back and forth over my sensitive bud, until I'm worried my legs will give out. I slide my fingers through his hair before holding on to his shoulders.

I moan loudly as he sucks my clit into his mouth, swirling his tongue in a maddeningly delicious rhythm. The pleasure builds within me, threatening to consume me completely. Although what he's doing is not so different from what he did at the wedding, it feels so different. I feel closer to him now. I feel like I know him better. I trust him... more.

"Fuck," I cry out as the first waves of an orgasm crash over me. Ben holds me steady with one hand on my hip as he continues to devour me. I lose myself in the intensity of it all, enjoying every second of my release as it sets every nerve ending in my body on fire.

"Ben, I need you. I need more. I need you completely," I beg. Ben licks a trail back up over my tummy before cupping my face and kissing me hard. His tongue dips into my mouth and I moan. He walks me backwards until I feel the edge of the bed on the back of my legs.

I slide onto the mattress and get on all fours. Ben looks at me but doesn't stop me as I reach out and pull his shorts down. His dick springs free and points at me. I'm not sure what's come over me because I've always hated doing this but somehow, with Ben, I love it. I feel an incredible desire when he looks at me with a glow on his face.

"Are you sure?" he asks.

"Never been more sure." I'm about to reach out and cup his balls when I remember his injury. "Oh shit, is that even okay? Can you with bruised testicles?" *I swear if Smutty's antics fucked this up for me, no more tuna!*

"Doctor said I can have sex if I'm not in pain. I'm good, Amelia, but you don't have to." He softly slides a hand through my hair and I am tempted to rub up against it like a cat.

"I think I owe them a blow and an apology," I say in what I hope is a seductive voice. My cheeks are burning, and I'm just glad that the light is low in the room. I'm the most neurotic sex kitten there ever was. Before I grab his erection he bends down and kisses me.

"But first, there's something missing," he says against my skin, sending another flutter of desire through me.

He steps away and retrieves something from his bedside table. My eyes widen when I see what—a butt plug and a tube of lube. He remembered.

"Turn around and bend over," he instructs firmly but gently.

I do as he says, feeling a mix of excitement and nervousness making me breathe faster.

Ben stands behind me and runs his hands over my bum, squeezing and kneading the flesh. "Such beautiful curves," he murmurs appreciatively.

I can't help but let out a soft moan at his touch, my body craving more.

He leans down and places a kiss on each cheek before spreading them apart, exposing my tight little hole to him.

"Relax," he says soothingly, "I'm going to prepare you," as he slides one finger in to spread some lube.

I take a deep breath and try to relax as I feel the cool metal of the plug against my skin. Ben coats it in lube before slowly pressing it against me.

"Fuck," I gasp as I feel myself being stretched around it.

"Relax, Amelia," he chides gently. "If it's too much you let me know."

"Yes, sir," I reply breathlessly.

He continues to push the plug into me until it pushes past my tight ring and is fully inside me with just the flared end nestling between my butt cheeks. I can't help but let out a low moan at the feeling of fullness.

"Good girl," he murmurs approvingly as he stands up and admires his handiwork. "Now, let's see how you look; stand up, darling."

I get up slowly and turn around to face him. The feeling of the plug inside me is both foreign and incredibly arousing. Every movement I make sends waves of pleasure radiating through my body.

"Twirl," he orders. "Bloody hell," he growls. "You look so fucking hot with that plug in your arse."

A blush creeps up my neck at his words, but at the same time they make me feel powerful and desired.

"Now then," he says, his voice dripping with lust and authority. "I think it's time for you to show me what a good little submissive you can be. And in return I'm going to show you what it means to be mine."

My breath catches in my throat at his words.

He reaches out and tangles his fingers in my hair, pulling gently until my head is tilted back and our eyes meet.

"You trust me?" he asks softly.

"Yes," I reply without hesitation.

"Good." He releases my hair and points for me to get back onto the bed. "Now suck my cock."

My pussy clenches at his words. I return to all fours before I reach out and wrap one hand around the base of his shaft. I look up at him for permission and when he nods I lean in and take the head of his cock into my mouth.

I start with slow, teasing licks, running my tongue over the sensitive tip. All the while I can feel the firm metal plug in my bum rubbing my sensitive nerve endings. Ben moans above me, and I feel a surge of pride at the sound. Encouraged by his reaction, I take him deeper, hollowing my cheeks as I suck.

"Fuck," he groans. "That's it, Darling. Take it all."

19

Breathe

Ben

I STAND AT THE foot of the bed and watch as Amelia, naked and on her knees, takes my cock into her mouth. She looks up at me with those big blue eyes, full of desire and lust. I thread my fingers through her hair, gripping it gently but firmly.

"That's it, Amelia," I say in a low voice. "Suck me off like a good girl."

She moans around my cock, the vibrations sending shivers down my spine. Her tongue swirls around the head as she takes me deeper. I can feel the heat of her mouth and the wetness that coats me as she works her way down.

"Fuck," I groan, unable to hold back. "That feels so fucking good."

Amelia looks up at me again, a smile playing on her lips. She pulls back slightly, letting her hand take over where her mouth left off. She pumps me slowly, teasingly.

"Is that what you want, sir?" she asks innocently.

I chuckle darkly. "Oh yes, that's exactly what I want." She returns her attention to my cock and I groan. I wish I could let her continue, but I need more and I know she does too. I reach down and pull her to up to me. My hands roam over her body as I kiss her deeply. I can taste myself on her tongue and it only fuels my desire.

"I need to fuck you," I growl against her lips. "I've waited so long for this." And I don't just mean since she came back into my life again. Somehow I feel like I've wanted to have her back in my arms ever since she walked away, all those years ago.

Amelia nods eagerly and slides back on the bed, spreading herself before me like an offering. Her pussy is glistening with arousal and I can't resist leaning in to taste her sweetness once more.

I bury my face between her thighs, licking and sucking at her clit while two fingers plunge deep inside of her. She moans and writhes beneath me, hips bucking against my hand.

"Yes! Oh my god, yes!" she cries out.

I continue to devour her until she's on the edge of orgasm before pulling away abruptly. I grab a condom from the bedside table and quickly roll it on, desperate to be inside of her. I position myself at her entrance and push in slowly, savouring the feeling of her tight heat around me. Amelia's nails dig into my shoulders as I fill her completely. I am where I need to be.

"Fuck, you feel so good," I groan. I give her a moment to adjust before I start to move, thrusting in and out with increasing urgency. Our bodies slap together with each motion, the sound echoing through the room. I lean forward, capturing one of Amelia's nipples between my teeth and bite down gently, tugging at it with my lips before releasing it with a pop. She gasps and arches into me, urging me on.

"Harder," she moans. "Please, Ben, harder." Hearing her call my name rather than "sir" almost pushes me over the edge. This is her and me, Amelia and Ben; not just a dom and his sub.

I grip her tightly and pick up the pace, slamming into her over and over again. The headboard bangs against the wall with each thrust, but neither of us cares about anything except the pleasure we share.

My hand wraps around Amelia's throat, applying just enough pressure to heighten her arousal. Her eyes roll back in ecstasy as she clings to the edge of release.

"That's it," I growl. "Be a good girl and come for me."

Her walls clench around me as she shatters beneath me, orgasm washing over her. The sight is too much for me and I bury myself deep within her as I find my own release.

We collapse onto the bed in a tangle of limbs and heavy breathing. My heart is pounding in my chest as I press a kiss to Amelia's forehead. I remember what it was like when we were young but this, just now, was ten thousand times better.

"BEN?" AMELIA'S VOICE ECHOES through the dark room. She's curled up in my arms. I'm a little sad because her scent is covered by the smell of my shower gel. After we caught our breath I took her to the bathroom for a rinse down. She blushed beetroot red when I pulled the butt plug from her bum. I couldn't hold back a chuckle. She is adorable when she turns from sexy little kitten into shy cat lady, and I'm not sure which of the two sides of the coin I adore more.

"Yes, darling?" I place a soft kiss on her shoulder.

"Thank you." She snuggles deeper into my embrace.

"What for?"

"For making me feel special." My heart breaks a little. What I want to say is "I love you." But I also know, if I say it now, she'll think I'm only saying it because of what she told me earlier. She won't believe me, and I don't think I can cope with her thinking I'm lying if I tell her the one thing that is truer to me than anything else.

"Any time." This is a truth I can share at least.

"Is there anything I can do for you?" Her fingers are gently stroking over the arm I have draped over her side.

"Ha, darling, do you think this wasn't also amazing for me?" I chuckle.

"Maybe, but I still want to do something you want to do. Tell me!" Amelia turns in my arms so she can look up at me.

"Go on a date with me."

"What?" she whispers barely audible.

"Let me take you on a real date, Amelia. That's what I want more than anything else." I hold her gaze and my heart hammers like crazy.

"And then?"

"If we have fun on the date, maybe let me take you out on another one." I cup her face. "You are an amazing woman and I'd like to give this another try. I know I hurt you back then. I fucking hurt you and I will try to make it up to you every day. I am no longer the boy I was twenty years ago; I know what I want from life and you are what I want the most." *I love you.* I want to add these three words so badly, but not yet. She's not ready.

There is a tiny frown on her face and I get ready for her to turn me down.

"I can agree to the date. I can't promise anything more at this point." The fear in her voice confirms what I assumed. She still doesn't trust me fully and I get it.

I press my lips to hers and pull her into a passionate kiss. My tongue slides alongside hers before licking the corners of her mouth. My lips brush over hers and nip and lick like this is the last chance I'll ever get to kiss her.

A MELIA'S BREATHING IS STEADY. Her hand holds onto the arm I've draped over her. It didn't take her long to fall asleep, but given that she had two mind-blowing orgasms it's not surprising.

A gentle scraping on the door breaks the silence in the room. Amelia reacts to the noise and curls up further but she doesn't wake up. I carefully slide out from under the duvet before tucking her back in. I grab my boxers from the floor and slip them and open the door.

"What do you want, Furball?" I whisper at the dark shadow in the corridor. He gives me a pitiful meow before sprinting a few steps towards the stairs. When he notices I'm not following he looks back and meows again.

I sigh, " Fine, lead the way cat."

I gently close the bedroom door and follow him through the dark house to the kitchen. He blinks at me when I switch on the light.

"Right, what would you like today? We have...", I reach for the first tin, "...Sauce Lover with Salmon or Beef in Gravy." *Fuck, they actually sound delicious*. Furball makes it clear he couldn't care less which one, he just wants it now. He weaves in and out between my legs and keeps licking me.

"Hey, stop that otherwise I'll tell Amelia that you made me feed you when it wasn't really time," I gently try to push him away with my foot but he takes it as an invitation to nibble my toes. I rush to scoop his food onto a plate and place it on the plastic mat next to the kitchen counter. He storms to it and swallows the first piece before he's even come to a full stop.

Leaning against the kitchen counter, I watch the black furball devour his food.

I love Amelia; I'm not sure if I ever stopped, but the love is definitely back. And stronger than ever. I just hope I don't mess it up again.

20

Mamma Mia

Amelia

A WALL OF NOISE greets me when I step into the coffee shop. *Ooooh that's new.* I haven't been here in a while (due to mission "avoid the Whitcombs," because this coffee shop is close to Ben and Fi's houses). They've clearly invested in some renovations since my last visit, and with their comfy sofa groups and trendy art on the wall they look more like a Shoreditch artisan coffee shop than the old, dated village caff I remember.

I join the queue whilst eyeing the different tables. The free one in the far corner is my target, and I pray nobody ahead of me snatches it up. I hate sitting in the centre of a room and given that that's where most tables are free I assume I'm not the only one.

The woman in front of me turns, clearly also trying to spot the best seat, and I notice the subtle logo on the T-shirt. Purr Inn. Right underneath is a name badge pinned to the material. It reads Bri—

"Oh my god, you're Bridget!" I exclaim. She studies me for a moment.

"Sorry, have we met before?" She sounds confused, and rightly so.

"No, yes, I called your cattery a few weeks back looking for emergency accommodation for my cat. I'm Amelia." I hold out my hand. She shakes it with a big grin on her face.

"Oh, I remember. Smutty, right?" I nod enthusiastically. "Did you find somewhere for him to stay?"

"Yes, a... friend took him. Sorry, I couldn't really afford your space."

"Don't worry," she waves me off, "I only work there. I've told the owner we are too expensive but she insists the rich twats in this area can afford it." *I like her!*

"Next!" The barista is impatiently waving Bridget forward.

After she's placed her order I pay for my latte and croissant.

"So, do you live here?" I ask as I join Bridget at the other end of the counter where our coffees are being prepared. I'm not sure what's come over me. I don't tend to chat with strangers but I feel a connection with her.

"I do. I moved here a little less than a year ago after my divorce," she says, shaking the little sugar sachet in her hand.

"Oh, I'm sorry."

"I'm not. It wasn't a happy marriage in the end," she shrugs, but even though she's making light of the situation there's something in her eyes that tells me it wasn't quite as painless as she's making out.

"Me and my husband... ex-husband... lived in the same village in Hampshire since we started dating twenty-four years ago, so I thought I needed a change when it was all over. An aunt of mine lives in a nursing home close to here so I knew the village and always liked it... I'm sorry, verbal diarrhoea alert," she says embarrassed. "Outside of work I don't really know many people here yet."

She takes her coffee from the barista.

"Do you want to join me and my friends... who are late as usual," I grin. "We all grew up here, but I'm the only one left living in Hadlow."

"I don't want to intrude."

"Not at all," I assure her just as my coffee is placed on the counter.

We head to the table I had declared my territory earlier.

"So, how is Smutty? Great name, by the way," she grins, taking a seat on the sofa. I follow suit and immediately regret my decision. The sofa is so soft that it feels like it's swallowing me up. Getting up with any kind of dignity will be a miracle.

"Living his best life. He loves that he now gets double attention from me and Ben, my... friend, bending to his will," I snort.

"They are little dictators, aren't they? I have a tabby one. Bella knows what she wants and she knows I'll give it to her." She giggles.

"And yet we love them," I sigh and we both nod in agreement.

"Sorry we're late," Miranda interrupts us as she drops into one of the chairs. Bea waves from the counter where she is ordering their coffees.

"No problem. Miranda, this is Bridget," I introduce them.

"Bri, please," my new friend corrects me. Yes, I think she's a new friend. Sometimes you meet someone and you just click.

We chitchat on how Bri and I met until Bea joins us.

"So, you and Ben snogging at Miranda's wedding was a surprise. Are you dating?" Bea gets straight to the point.

"Friend, huh?" Bri giggles. I can feel my cheeks heat up.

"We're not 'dating' dating." Even I don't know what that means, but I can't really tell them that he's just introducing me to my submissive side. And then there's the date he's taking me on tomorrow. So, maybe we are dating. *Oh fuck! We are DATING.*

"No? So, what are you? I can't believe Ben is into that kinky stuff. Is he forcing you to do any of that shit?" Bea asks, and for a moment I think she's genuinely concerned for me. But of course, she can't help herself and keeps talking. "I mean, he told you he thinks you are ug... not attractive, so it can't be that."

"Bea!" Miranda exclaims and I shift uncomfortably in my chair.

"Well, it's true. He was such an arse back then. I'm not sure why your husband is still friends with him." Bea stares Miranda down before taking another sip.

"People change," I try to interject causing Bea to roll her eyes.

"I know it's none of my business, but what exactly happened?" Bri asks.

"She and Ben dated twenty years ago. She overheard him telling people that he was only with her until someone better came along," Bea says casually, but it almost sounds like she is enjoying it.

"And now he hit her up on some kinky BDSM app and is dating her." She finishes it.

"It's not that simple," I mutter.

"What did I miss, Amelia? I'm just a bit worried about you," she says, but it's not coming across as genuine. Or maybe I'm just avoiding facing up to it?

"He only got in touch to explain what went down before and to say sorry. The whole dating thing just... well, it sort of happened. It wasn't part of his grand plan."

"Oh, Amelia. I'll give you that he's a dreamboat on paper, with the looks and the dosh, but he's not your Mr. Right. He's probably just playing you again," Bea sighs.

"Wait, let me get this straight," Bri interrupts. "He's fit, loaded, and can have any woman he fancies. Why bother going through the hassle of apologizing and dating her if he's not properly interested? In my book, blokes don't go to that much trouble if they're not keen."

Bea gives Bri a nasty look.

"I'm with Bri," Miranda interjects, catching Bea off guard. Miranda always backs Bea so this is a bit of a curveball. "I mean, he didn't need to reach out at all. And I saw you two at my wedding: he was absolutely smitten with you. Did he tell you why he messed up back then?"

I shoot Miranda a grateful smile before delving into Ben's apology. When I recount how Ben rescued Smutty and then me, the others all sigh with glee. Well, all except Bea.

"I'm not buying it. Sorry, Amelia," she snaps.

"Bea, what's the issue? What's getting under your skin about this? Are you telling me you haven't changed in twenty years? We all made mistakes when we were young. Sure, he messed up big time back then, and it hurt me. I haven't forgotten that. But he's not the same man he was. He's changed."

"Women in abusive relationships always say that." Bea snorts.

"I'm not just any 'woman,' and I'm not in an abusive relationship," I assert, surprisingly resolute. Usually I shy away from standing up to her. "Why are you so dead-set against him being right for me? Is it that YOU think he's too good-looking for me?"

"Of course not," she laughs nervously. "I'm just looking out for you. But if you don't want my advice I won't bother." She theatrically glances at her watch before rising from her chair. "I've got to run. Nice meeting you, Bri," she mutters, barely giving us a glance before storming out of the coffee shop.

We sit there in a shock for a moment before Bri breaks the silence.

"She's watched too many Hollywood high school dramas."

I T WAS A FUN afternoon after Bea left. I think we made a new friend in Bri, and we have already agreed to meet up for dinner in the next few weeks.

And Bea, well, I won't reach out first this time. Truth be told I'm not sure I want her to reach out either. We've have grown apart and maybe we just have to accept the fact that we once were friends but no longer are. Does that make me a cold-hearted bitch or just a realist?

I have a big smile on my face as I unlock the door to Ben's house and step into the warmth. Noises from the TV drift down the corridor but otherwise there is no sound in the house.

"Ben," I call out whilst toeing off my shoes. He appears in the door to the living room, Smutty right next to him. Both look like they just woke up. Adorable is not a strong enough word for them.

"Did you nap with Smutty?" I smirk.

"No," he replies, trying to look innocent. "I fell asleep watching the game."

"And Smutty?"

"Fell asleep on my chest," he grins before pulling me into his arms for a kiss. *Oh wow,* and what a kiss it is. He pushes me up against the wall and nips and sucks on my lips like there's no tomorrow. When he takes a step back I feel woozy.

"Good afternoon with the girls?" he asks as he pulls me with him into the living room, Smutty hot on our heels because he hasn't received his pats yet.

"I made a new friend," I reply, nuzzling Smutty to my chest. His purring has its usual relaxing influence on me. "So, tell me, the date tomorrow. What are we doing?"

"Top Secret," he grins. "But wear a nice dress." He winks.

Oh, the wink again. He is killing me.

21

Serenade No.13

Amelia

I FIDGET AS THE car travels along the A23 towards Brighton. I'm so excited. Ben's not just taking me on a date: he's taking me on an epic date. It took me a bit more probing and a lot of kissing to finally get it out of him. But in the end, he cracked and spilled the beans.

We are going to a candlelit concert of my favourite composition by Mozart. I can't believe it, but he remembered how much I love "*Eine kleine Nachtmusik.*" I'm not generally a classical fan but Mozart is my go-to music when I need to calm down after a busy day.

"We should be there in half an hour, sir." I bite back my giggle when Omar addresses him as sir. Suddenly the word has a completely different feel to it. Ben eyes me and winks. I'm sure he knows exactly what's going through my head.

"Thank you, Omar," he replies. I straighten my dress a bit. I have been working from home as it's Friday and sneakily booked in a two-hour meeting with Samira at the end of the day, which I used to model different outfits for her on Zoom. I'm not a girly girl by any stretch of the imagination so my wardrobe is limited, but eventually I found a dress I wore three years ago to someone's wedding and by a miracle it fit and actually looks quite sexy. It's black, has an A-line skirt, and shows just enough of my chest to transform it from dreary to daring. I also played around with a chiffon scarf and used it to tie my hair back in a way that looks playful but elegant (Samira's words). When Ben, who had been at the office all day, picked me up from his house, he almost dragged me off to the bedroom for a quickie, which I took as a good sign.

Ben's hand is gently stroking my knee. I've already had to push his hand back down twice because it was wandering up under my skirt and I won't let him finger me here, right next to his driver. We are only in an SUV after all, not a limousine where we can shut ourselves away. I peek at the books on the passenger seat next to Omar.

"What are you studying?" The titles of the books don't sound familiar.

"A Master's in Development Studies, I'm in my last year," he confirms with a proud smile on his face. I try to judge how old he is. He doesn't look much younger than we are.

"That's so exciting."

"I think so. Lots of people don't understand why I started to study this late in life, but I believe it's never too late to do the things you want," he grins.

"Couldn't agree more," Ben mumbles. I look at him but his gaze is directed at the window. Did he mean us or the direction he's taking his company in?

When we reach Brighton Pavilion my jaw almost drops like in one of those silly cartoons. I had heard about the building but had never seen it in the flesh, so to speak. Talk about a place that screams 'fancy.' The sparkling white minarets and domes give off serious fairytale vibes, making me wonder if I've accidentally stepped into a magical realm. The building looks like an Indian or Oriental palace and carries an air of *One Thousand and One Nights.* We stop at the entrance to the garden, and I'm sure in the summer it's filled with flowers. Now, at the end of February, it's almost bare, with the odd spring flower coming through, but it's not difficult to imagine the place in bloom.

"This is amazing," I whisper as Ben helps me out of the car. He waves off Omar, who will set himself up in a coffee shop somewhere to study, and takes my hand.

"It is, isn't it." He agrees and gives me a warm smile before cupping my face and kissing me. I don't think there's been a minute since we left where he hasn't touched me. It's like he needs the contact to make sure I'm really here.

"And the concert is in the Pavilion?" I wonder what it will look like on the inside.

"Yes, come on." He pulls me through the main entrance. Ben is wearing a dark suit and he looks hot. Truth be told, I like him in his casual clothes, but jeez Louise he looks delicious in formal wear.

"Good evening, sir," the usher welcomes us. I giggle and Ben gently squeezes my hand. We are directed along a corridor decorated almost entirely in red and gold until we get to some open double doors. Outside them is a small bar and next to the doors is a sign saying *Music Room*. "Darling, before we go in, I want you to take this. Go to the Ladies room and put it in." Ben holds out a velvet bag the size of my hand.

"What is it," I ask as I reach for it. When my fingers close around it, I feel the outline of the item in the bag and blush. "Ben!" I hiss.

He chuckles and places a kiss on my nose. "Be a good girl and put it in so you can have some public play," he whispers. He remembered that as well. I give him another look before heading towards the toilets obediently.

Heat is pooling between my legs, and I hope that means I'm getting wet because I'm going to need the lubrication.

I carefully push the door open and listen. Nobody else seems to be in the loos and so I quickly slip into the first cubical and lock the door. I take a seat on the toilet. Might as well pee whilst I'm here.

I peek into the bag and see a weird u-shaped vibrator. I have seen them before but they confuse me so I've never ordered one. I stick to my classic rabbit.

Just when I pull it from the bag someone stomps into the Ladies room and I almost drop the vibrator. I freeze on the toilet with the sex toy in my hand. God, please don't let there be an emergency or something right now. The person takes the cubical next to me and starts to pee loudly. I heard a horse pee once and it wasn't as loud. Eventually my cubical neighbour flushes the toilet and heads out of the bathroom. Without washing her hands, I'd like to add.

I return my focus to the vibrator and try to work out which end goes where. Maybe it doesn't matter as they look almost identical. One end is a bit flatter than the other, but that's the only difference I can see.

Me

I don't know how this works?

I stare at my phone and wait. I can see when Ben reads my message because the tick turns blue but he doesn't reply. *Bastard!*

I'm about to give up and just try it when there's a knock on the door to the toilet before it's pushed open.

"Amelia?"

"Ben," I whisper shout. "You can't be here!"

"Open up," he demands from outside my cubical.

I rip the door open. "Ben!"

"Go in," he gently pushes me back into the cubical. I suddenly remember that I haven't flushed yet and slam the toilet seat lid shut in panic.

"Don't look." I hiss. Ben shakes his head at my antics and holds out his hand.

"Give me the vibrator." He demands and, like a good submissive would, I hand it over. *What's the point of pretending to fight him on this? I want this after all.*

"Lift your skirt."

"Ben, what if someone comes in?"

"I have an usher waiting outside. He thinks you're not feeling well," is all he says. I grab the hem and hold it up for him.

"Spread your legs, darling," he commands. I cautiously do as I'm told and he pulls my knickers from my body. He slips one end of the vibrator in his mouth before pulling it back out. I can see it glistening with his spit. He gently pushes the now wet end of the vibrator into my pussy. I gasp and my hands land on his shoulders to help to steady myself.

"Right, and this end goes here." He places the flat end against my clit. "How does it feel?" he asks.

"Full," that's really the only word I can describe it. It had looked so small in my hand, but inside me it's definitely noticeable. Frankly, I'm questioning how I'll be able to walk with it.

"Good." He kisses me and unlocks the cubical. "Let's go." I take a few steps from the confined space. Uh-oh, yup, I can definitely feel that. The part inside my pussy is rubbing against my inner wall whilst the flat bit gently slides over my clit. I carefully walk to the sink and wash my hands.

"Oh, wait." Ben steps back into the cubical and flushes the toilet. I'm mortified. I don't want to look in the mirror because I'm sure I'm as red as the corridor outside the toilet door.

"Come on, darling," he takes my hand and drags me out of the bathroom. A young guy with glasses looks at us.

"Thank you so much, she's feeling a lot better," Ben says smoothly and holds out a twenty-pound note for the usher. He thanks Ben profusely and shuffles off.

"You're crazy, I hope you know that," I whisper as I walk past him towards the doors to the music room. Suddenly there's strong vibration in my pussy and on my clit, and I almost topple over against the bar. I straighten myself and look at Ben.

"I'm in control, darling," he says and pulls out a little oval plastic thingy the same colour as the vibrator. He has a remote for it. *Oh shit!*

My HEART POUNDS WITH anticipation. We're seated on plush velvet seats in one of the most impressive rooms I have ever seen. It's an opulent and extravagant space showcasing intricate details and vibrant colours. Large glass chandeliers hang from the vaulted ceiling. The dome is covered in paintings and the walls are adorned with richly patterned wallpaper. Some of the pillars have snake ornaments on them and stained-glass windows allow light in. The edges of the room have been roped off, probably to stop people from touching the historic wallpaper.

Behind the rope hundreds of LED candles give a warm glow to the room. I assume this is a measure to reduce fire risk——who wants hundreds of open flames in a room like this?——, but artificial candles don't take away from the magical atmosphere. It is simply breathtaking.

Ben and I sit smack bang in the middle of the room and we are surrounded by people. I really hope he's not planning on using the vibrator here. I look over at Ben and he gives me a mischievous smile in response. A tingle of excitement runs through me. *Ahem, maybe I don't think it's a bad idea after all?*

The lights dim and members of a small orchestra step onto the stage. The opening notes of the first movement of Mozart's "*Eine Kleine Nachtmusik*" fill the room. This part of the serenade is fast-paced and I feel myself relax into my seat. The music is beautiful, each note floating through the air. I close my eyes and let it wash over me as a sense of calm settles in my chest.

But as I start to drift off into a world of music and daydreams I feel a gentle buzz against my clit. My eyes snap open and I look at Ben in surprise. He winks at me and reaches into his pocket, pulling out the small control.

I bite my lip as he presses another button on the remote, causing the buzzing sensation to intensify. I shoot him a playful glare before turning my attention back to the concert pretending that the vibrator isn't having an effect on me. The music swells around us. It's impossible not to get swept up in its beauty, but with each passing minute the vibrations against my sensitive flesh become more insistent. When the musicians speed up, Ben increases the vibrations. When they slow down, he does the same until the vibrations are barely noticeable.

I squirm in my seat trying to find some relief, but every shift just makes it worse. I shoot Ben a pleading look and he grins at me with a fire in his eyes. He knows exactly what he's doing to me.

Then the violins start to play faster and louder just as they approach the end of the movement. I can feel myself teetering on the edge of going insane. The vibrations are relentless now, sending shockwaves of pleasure through my body. I grip the armrests of my chair and try to hold on as everything inside me starts to unravel.

But just as I'm about to tip over into blissful release, the music stops. The room falls silent, and I let out a frustrated groan. Everyone around us claps politely, oblivious to the erotic torture I've been enduring.

Ben leans over and whispers in my ear, his voice low and husky: "Not yet."

I'm torn between frustration and arousal. The musicians on stage start to tune their instruments in preparation for the next movement and I realise this is far from over.

The next part of "*Eine Kleine Nachtmusik*" is slow paced and gentle. I wait for Ben to activate the vibrator, but nothing.

I try to focus on the music and make it through almost the entire piece when the vibrator starts to hum gently. Not much, but a little. Ben keeps it at this level all through movement two. But during the next piece, he ever so slowly increases the intensity, building up my frustration again. By the end of it I'm desperate for more.

"One more," he whispers as the first notes of the fourth and final movement ring out. It is another fast-paced one. It starts off with a melody imitating the singing of birds, and Ben presses another button on the remote control. I lean back in my seat and try to relax, but it's impossible to ignore the constant hum of pleasure radiating through my body. Each note seems to vibrate in perfect harmony with the toy inside me, intensifying the sensations until it's all I can think about.

I steal a glance at Ben who is watching me with lust and desire. He leans closer and brushes his lips against my ear.

"Imagine everyone watching you right now," he murmurs. "If they would only know that you are being a naughty girl desperate for me to let her come."

His words send a shiver down my spine as I picture it——a sea of faces turned towards me as I squirm in my seat, desperately trying not to moan or cry out in ecstasy.

"You're so close, Amelia," he continues. "But you can't let go just yet. You have to hold it together until we're alone."

His words ignite a desire within me as I cling to the edge of control. The vibrations against my clit and in my pussy are now relentless, pushing me closer and closer to the edge. The part inside me presses gently but firmly against my G spot, and as Ben increases the speed of the vibrations again, I almost lose it. A low moan escapes from deep within my throat before I can stop it, but thankfully it gets lost in the swell of sound around us.

As the final notes hang in the air like a promise unfulfilled I try to keep my composure. My body is wound tight with need, every nerve ending on high alert.

Ben's hand finds its way under my skirt and he grips my thigh possessively as he watches me. I'm so close now, teetering on the edge of a cliff, and I know that with just a little push I'll finally fall.

I meet his gaze and he nods as if he can read my thoughts. He hits a button on the remote and the strongest vibration so far hits me, and everything inside me unravels. I lean my head against his shoulder and press my lips together as wave after wave of ecstasy crashes over me. I grip Ben's hand tightly as I ride out the orgasm, lost in a myriad of feelings.

The room comes back into focus and I realise that we're still surrounded by people. But instead of being embarrassed or self-conscious, all I feel is a deep sense of satisfaction.

I let out a shuddering breath. My heart pounds in my chest as everyone around us gets to their feet to show their appreciation for the musicians.

I don't think I'll ever be able to listen to Mozart without thinking of Ben.

22

From Now On

Ben

AMELIA CLINGS TO ME as we walk out of the Music Room. I knew I had to wear the tightest boxer briefs I have today: my cock is hard and throbbing, and I can't wait to get her alone. I should have booked a hotel room in Brighton rather than having to make the one-hour drive back home. But Furball is on his own and I think he would have planned my murder if I kept Amelia from him for a whole night.

I'll miss him when they eventually move back to Amelia's cottage. But not as much as I'll miss her. I swallow hard and try to not let the thought ruin my evening. Luckily for me, her landlady's plumber is hopeless, so there's no date yet for her boiler to be fixed. So far I have been able to convince her to stay, even though the temperature is warmer now.

"Ben!" a familiar voice calls from behind me. "Ben, my boy, that's a coincidence." Shit! My eyes land on the short, balding man heading our way. He has an arm around a woman at least fifteen years his junior.

"Neil, that's a surprise." It really is a surprise because I'm pretty sure he once told me he hates classical music.

"Oh, you know, sometimes you have to do something nice for the wifey so she does something nice for you, if you get my gist." He winks and then laughs about his own joke. I give him a smirk and it takes everything in me not to roll my eyes.

"Amelia, this is Neil Blackwater from Henderson Steel Works. Coop and I are considering a collaboration with them," I introduce him. "Neil, this is Amelia Foley, my partner." I slide my hand around her waist. Amelia looks at me with surprise when I call her my partner, but relaxes into my embrace.

"Oh, don't play hard to get Ben. You know Henderson Steel is the leading manufacturer of steel beams in the country and your only real option," he laughs. "Nice to meet you, Amelia. You're not quite what I imagined Ben's girlfriend to look like," he laughs.

Arsehole! Amelia stiffens but I pull her closer to make it clear she's with me.

"In a good way, of course," Neil adds and lifts Amelia's hand to his mouth to place a phony kiss on it. Amelia flinches but allows him to press his lips to the back of her hand. Neil is in his late fifties and from an era when it was still considered okay to grope your secretary or make lude jokes in boardrooms. He's not a man I would choose to hang out with, were it not for the business deal.

"Did you like the concert, my dear?" Brenda, or Mrs Neil as her husband introduced her to us, asks Amelia.

"Oh, it was .... stimulating," she eventually replies with a cheeky smile. *That little minx.* I gently squeeze her side and she giggles.

Brenda clearly agrees with Amelia——albeit for completely different reason, I'm sure——as she gives us a short lecture about why Mozart is superior to all other composers. Amelia is squirming next to me probably because by now she is keen to take the vibrator out. I'm tempted to switch it on one more time. She was so beautiful coming apart earlier when she tried not to be obvious; it took everything in me not to whisk her away in the middle of the concert.

"Oh, you must," I suddenly hear Brenda say. *Shit, what did I miss?*

"If my little wifey says so, you can't possibly not, Ben. If we talk about the deal we can write off the dinner as a business expense," Neil chuckles. *Fuck, no!* That's the last thing I want now. Dinner with Neil and his wife.

"I—"

"Of course, we would love to join you for dinner," Amelia says. I give her a quick look and she just shrugs.

"Excellent," Neil slaps my back and I have to suppress the urge to slap him back.

"The restaurant is just across the street. The Duck and Orange. We'll meet you there." He gives us one last smirk and then drags his wife off after him.

"Amelia, why—"

"It sounded important, with the deal and everything." She looks at me nervously. "Should I not have accepted?"

"Honestly I'd much rather take you home and give you another orgasm than sit through a dinner with these people," I whisper and plant a kiss on her lips. *Fuck, I think I'm addicted to her.* "I also don't think Furball is going to forgive us."

"Oh my god, you do care about Smutty!" she exclaims with a big grin.

"I——well, it will be me he'll bite on the ankle again if we're late," I argue, but we both know it's a weak excuse. Yes, that little black shadow has grown on me.

"Sure," she smirks. "Well we can use Omar waiting for us as an excuse to not stay too long," she shrugs. "But before we go, I'll have to nip to the ladies because this thing needs to come out." An older woman walking pass stares at us curiously causing Amelia to blush again. I wonder if she'll ever get used to her new sexy kitten side, but I sure hope not. I love her pink cheeks.

T HIS FEELS LIKE THE longest dinner ever when in reality only forty-five minutes have passed. Normally I would be all over business partners——anything to make the deal happen——but today I'm bored by the business talk and all I want to do is get Amelia home and bury myself in her.

Maybe Coop is right. Maybe we have done this all-work-and-no-fun thing long enough. It's time to enjoy life a little.

"Would you excuse me, I'll just head to the bathroom," Amelia says and slides from her chair. She gives me a smile and disappears behind the screen separating our table from the next. It's a weird restaurant. They've got wooden partitions between each table, making it feel like you've got your own little bubble. The menu sounds posh but if you look closely it's just overpriced chicken.

"Amelia's nice," Neil takes a sip of his whiskey, "but definitely not who I would have pictured you with."

I hold his gaze. "And why's that?"

"Oh, it's just that you're so successful... well, don't listen to me. I'm an old man," he chuckles. "My father was very strict and always made it clear we need to choose our partners carefully so they don't hold us back."

I glance at his wife, but she's not listening and instead is clicking away on her phone with her acrylic nails.

"And you think Amelia's holding me back?" My voice sounds dangerous.

"Oh, don't listen to me. I just have the old-fashioned notion that a successful man needs to be supported by a beautiful woman. As I said, I'm just a relic from a different time."

He did not just say that to me! I try to calm my breathing before I reply.

"And what you're saying is that Amelia isn't beautiful?" My eyes are fixed on him and the mood around the table is shifting.

"Oh... I——" I don't think he expected me to call him out on his shit. I need to get out of here before I do something wrong.

I drop my napkin on the table and slowly rise from my chair.

"Neil, unfortunately our company is no longer interested in a partnership with you." I pronounce each word clearly and display a calmness I don't feel on the inside.

"Let's not be hasty, Ben. I didn't mean to offend and I apologise if I have." Neil tries to calm the waters.

"Amelia is a beautiful and amazing woman; she is smart, caring, and makes me happy. I tell you what she isn't: she is not a trophy I drag along with me. You might not have wanted to offend, Neil, but this conversation has shown me your values and they're not values that match what Coop and I want for our company."

Neil's face is turning crimson and his smile is slipping off his face. All that's left now is resentment and anger. I know how desperate his company is for this deal, regardless of the stupid delaying games he's been playing.

"Think, Ben. You're giving up the chance of signing a contract with the market leader. We can help you maximise your profits, we can make this project a real success. Are you really throwing it all away over a fat wallflower with no style?" Our eyes are locked and neither of us moves. I have never felt fury quite like this.

"Fuck your company. And fuck your deal," I hiss. The anger burns in my guts like a wildfire and it takes every ounce of strength for me not to punch the shit out of this wanker. "There are many other companies around, and if we can't find a partner in the UK, we'll take our business elsewhere. But I won't be making deals with someone who's got the manners of a chauvinistic arsehole." I snatch Amelia's bag. "Excuse me." I give a nod to Brenda and stride off to find Amelia.

I sidestep the screen guarding our table and nearly collide with her. Her expression is blank, she seems to be frozen on the spot. I'm sure she heard what was said.

"Let's go, darling," I whisper and place a kiss on her lips. She takes the hand I hold out to her and we leave the restaurant without a backwards look.

23

Man On A Mission

Amelia

NEITHER OF US HAS said a word the whole drive home. Ben held my hand but his attention was elsewhere. He was probably worried about the business. I cost him a massive deal! I should be elated that he defended me but I worry that Neil may have been right.

I mean, open any magazine. Successful men don't have women like me on their arm.

When we got home Smutty demanded our full attention until he had his fill of cuddles. Now he's lying on his bed, exhausted from all the purring.

"Want a drink?" Ben asks and holds up a glass bottle with a golden liquid in it.

"No, thanks." In the two weeks I've stayed at Ben's I haven't seen him drink whiskey. Occasionally he'll have a beer with his dinner but he doesn't seem to be a big drinker.

"Ben, I'm sorry." I whisper. One of us has to bring the situation up, right? "I'm really sorry." I fight back tears. I hate that he lost a deal because of me.

Ben places his glass to the counter.

"What are you sorry for?" There is a deep frown on his face and I'm not sure if he's upset with me. He takes his suit jacket off and pulls off his tie .

"That you lost the deal because of me. I mean I appreciate that you defended me, but he wasn't that wro—" He pulls me into his arms and stops me from talking with a long kiss. I can taste the smokiness of his drink when his tongue dips into my mouth and I have to fight back a moan. *That man can kiss!*

"No, Amelia." He cups my face in his hands. "No. Don't you say sorry to me. You have nothing to be sorry about. You're who I want at my side, not as my trophy but as my partner. And anyone who can't see how amazing you are can fuck right off." There is so much conviction in his voice. I'm still waiting for him to do something that tells me he was just pulling the wool over my eyes. But what he did today was a grand gesture. No, I shouldn't call it that because that would mean he did it all just for the effect. No, he meant it; he truly meant it. How could I doubt him?

I close the distance between us and press my mouth to his. I kiss him with everything I have, hoping to show him how I feel about him.

"I need to make love to you, Amelia," he whispers. There is something soul shattering in his eyes. This is not about sex or pleasure; this is about being as close to each other as possible. I take his hand in mine and lead the way to the bedroom.

Our steady breath is the only noise in the house. But it's not an uncomfortable silence, it's a silence that tells me that the world and all its ugliness is out there, but in here, it's just us.

When the door slams shut I turn around and study Ben. He looks intense, like a man on a mission.

"Let me help you." I take a step towards him. My gaze is fixed on the buttons of his shirt as I undo each one slowly, slipping my fingers in the gaps between them, brushing against his skin. It's so warm under there; my own skin feels like it's beginning to burn.

When I get to the last button I ease the shirt off his shoulders slowly, deliberately brushing my fingers against his muscles as I pull it down past his elbows and wrists. It drops to the floor with a faint thud. Ben manoeuvres around me and takes a seat on the bed.

"Take your dress off," he demands.

This dress doesn't have a zip and so I awkwardly lift it over my head and throw it on top of his shirt. I hesitate for a moment, but when I see Ben's burning look, I remove my bra and knickers with as much grace as I can muster.

My eyes never leave Ben's, not even when he briefly stands up and removes his own trousers and underwear.

"Come here." He holds out his hand. I follow his invitation and straddle his lap. He kisses me with tender longing; it's a soft and gentle kiss that reaches into the very depths of my being. The sensations he invokes are overwhelming; it feels like all my senses are on high alert.

I moan softly when his hands slide down to cup my bum and squeeze gently. It's such a simple action but it sends shockwaves through my body. We break apart to gaze at each other, our lips just inches apart.

"You're fucking gorgeous," Ben tells me in no uncertain terms before capturing my lips with his once more.

The kiss deepens as he urges me onto my back on the bed, following closely behind until he is lying half on top of me. His hips slot between mine as our tongues tangle together in an exhilarating dance of need and desire.

Ben grinds his hard length against my pussy, driving us both into a frenzy of lust for one another. He pulls back from the kiss to trail hot open-mouthed kisses down the side of my neck making me gasp out loud.

"Mine." The single word rumbles through Ben's chest.

"Yes, yours," I pant out breathlessly as heat pools low in my belly at his claim over my body.

I WAKE UP to the sound of water coming from the bathroom. I blink a few times and focus my eyes on the open door. Ben is shaving in just his boxer shorts——huh, sexy. I reach for my nighty on the chair next to the bed and slip it on. We have given up the pretence that I'm staying in the guest room and my belongings are now spread out in his bedroom.

"Morning," I say and place a kiss on his naked shoulder as I grab my toothbrush.

"Morning, darling."

"I can't hear any noise from His Lordship."

"I fed him when I got up. He was already pacing like a puma in the corridor," Ben grins before dragging the shaver over his cheeks again.

"You do realise that you're his submissive," I giggle.

"Only to him," he winks before wiping the last of his shaving foam off as I rinse my mouth. "Can I get a minty fresh morning kiss then?" He pulls me into his arms.

"Ben, don't you want breakfast?" I try to protest.

"It's just after seven. Furball has been fed. We could climb back into bed for a bit?" he wiggles his eyebrows.

"We're not bunnies," I laugh, but at the same time I have to hold myself back from jumping him like a cat in heat at the thought of yet another amazing orgasm. How many has it been in the last twenty-four hours. Three, four?

He can read me like a book and knows he's won. Smiling, he leans in, his lips lingering against mine as he deepens the kiss. I wrap my arms around him and pull him closer, losing myself in the sensation of his mouth on mine.

His hands start to wander lower down my body, stroking my sides before moving up to cup my breasts through the thin fabric of my nightie. My nipples harden instantly under his touch sending a jolt of desire straight to my core.

I moan softly into his mouth as his hands continue their exploration, sliding down over my stomach to rest between my thighs. He presses his palm against me, applying just the right amount of pressure to make me gasp with pleasure.

"I want you," he whispers against my lips, his voice husky with desire.

I look into his eyes and see raw passion burning in them. I can feel my own desire building with each passing second until it's all-consuming, leaving no room for rational thought.

"Yes!"

He nods and walks me back to the bed.

"Bend over," he demands. Oh goody, my PD is here.

"Yes, sir," I reply and place my arms on the mattress. Ben grabs a condom from the bedside table and slides it on as he walks back to me.

"Stunning," he groans as his finger slides along my spine before he cups my backside with both of his hands.

"This will be a quick one, Amelia, since you want breakfast," he chuckles. *Bastard!*

He leans down to kiss my neck as he positions himself and slides his hard cock into my burning pussy. This is an angle we haven't tried before, and I like it. Every thrust hits me just right, just where I want it. My breath catches in my throat at the exquisite sensation of being filled by him once more and I cling tightly to the sheet as he begins to move.

His thrusts are slow and deep at first, gradually increasing in speed and intensity as we become lost in our shared passion. The room is filled with the sound of our moans mingling as we move as one.

I feel a familiar tightening deep inside me that tells me I'm getting close, and I know Ben is too from his ragged breathing.

"Rub your clit, Amelia," he orders.

"Yes, sir," I gasp and moan out loud when I draw the first circle around the swollen nub.

The combination of my fingers on my clit and his hard cock pounding into me is enough to send me hurtling over the edge. I cry out his name as my orgasm crashes over me, my body shaking with the force of it.

He follows me a few seconds later, his hips jerking forward as he spills himself into the condom with a hoarse cry.

I crawl under the duvet and Ben follows me once he has disposed of the condom. We lie in each other's arms, breathing heavily as we come down from our shared high.

"I love you," he says softly, breaking the silence. I pull him to me and kiss him. I can't say the words. Not yet.

Something is holding me back but I hope the kiss is enough to show him that I am his and his alone.

24

All Of Me

Ben

"WANT MORE JUICE?" AMELIA peeks around the fridge door. She is wearing an oversized T-shirt that hangs to mid-thigh. Her hair is in a messy bun and she has fluffy pink socks on. She looks so delicious and what I really want is her and not sodding orange juice.

I grin. "Yes, sure."

"Why are you looking at me like that?" She pours juice in my glass and slides on the stool next to me.

"You look mouth-watering," I place soft kisses on her neck and nibble on her earlobe. My hand slides under her shirt. I can't get enough of her.

"Ben! Not again! Have some self-restraint." Her protest is followed by a moan as I pinch her nipple. I'm about to take her shirt off when the doorbell chimes.

"Who's that?" she whispers between kisses.

"Don't know, but they can bugger off," I gently bite her bottom lip but the arsehole at the door doesn't get the message. Whoever it is now has their finger on the bell nonstop .

"Fuck," I swear and get off the stool. "Stay here," I order.

"Are you mad, look what I'm wearing?" Before I can stop her, she slips pass me and runs up the stairs. I shake my head.

"Hold your horses," I shout and pull open the door. I'm faced with Coop. His face is thunderous. "Hey."

"What. The. Actual. Fuck. Ben!" he shouts and for one moment I'm worried he'll punch me. But then he gets a hold of himself. It helps that Lizzie puts a calming hand on his back.

"Maybe come in and shout at me inside, so you don't give my neighbours a reason to gossip," I exhale and head back to the kitchen. I have a suspicion I know what that is about.

"Want a cuppa?" I ask Coop and Lizzie as they join me in the kitchen. Lizzie grins and gives me a thumbs up but Coop is just glaring at me.

"I take it Neil called you?" I ask tentatively.

"What the fuck, Ben! Why did you cancel the deal? You could have at least spoken with me about it. I can't believe this! We have been business partners for over fifteen years and friends even longer, and you just go and cancel a major deal without even talking to me."

Furball shoots into the kitchen and sits down next to me as if to protect me.

"Oh, that cat is adorable," Lizzie coos and bends down to stroke him. My bodyguard immediately surrenders his protective position and drops on his side for some patting from her.

"Sugar?" I ask Lizzie and she nods. She and I know we need to let Coop vent. He hardly ever loses his cool, and when he does, he just needs to vent.

"Hello? Is anyone listening to me? Ben, forget the freaking tea and tell me what the fuck happened," he shouts even louder with his arms crossed.

"Coop—"

"It's my fault." Amelia stands in the doorway pulling nervously on the black T-shirt she's wearing with yoga pants. It has a grey cat emblazed on it and the slogan "I'm purrrrr-fect"

"I'm sorry, Coop," she sniffles.

"Amelia," Coop's expression changes immediately and he gives her one of his signature grins before pulling her into a hug. "How are you?" Apparently our argument is over. That's why Lizzie calls him her teddy bear. He couldn't harm a fly with that heart of gold.

"I'm okay. I'm really sorry." She looks from him to me and I hold out my arms. She crosses the kitchen and cuddles against my chest. I love that she sees me as a place of safety now.

"Ben? What happened?" His anger has been replaced with worry.

"Neil disrespected Amelia." I leave it there as I don't want to repeat the hurtful words that wanker muttered.

"He called me a fat wallflower with no taste, and Ben cancelled the deal," Amelia says quietly.

"Motherfucker," Lizzie hisses and I have to bite back a laugh. Lizzie says it as it is. Always.

"I told him he shouldn't have done that just because of me," Amelia sniffles.

"Yes, he should have!" Lizzie exclaims.

"What did you tell him?" Coop asks me.

"Fuck your company. And fuck your deal." I shrug. I don't regret a word of what I said.

A big grin appears on Coop's face. " Good. Oh, and sorry for shouting. I should have known."

"You should have," I agree, "But I should have given you a heads up as well." Truth is the conversation with Neil left me raging with anger and then worried about how Amelia felt. I completely forgot to message Coop.

"Neil called me first thing this morning and said I needed to talk to you because you lost your marbles yesterday and cancelled the deal for no apparent reason." He slides onto one of the stools and takes a piece of the toast I haven't finished.

"I guess you're joining us," I chuckle and point at the bread in his hand.

"Hey, he called me in the middle of making breakfast. I have some half-cooked eggs sitting on my cooker."

"He barely gave me time to get dressed." Lizzie rolls her eyes before waving at Amelia, "I'm Lizzie, by the way. This lunatic's girlfriend."

"Fiancé," Coop corrects her and pinches her in her side making her squeal and jump. Amelia giggles against my chest. This right here is why we need to step back and make time for things other than work.

"Ben, you did the right thing." Coop says before taking another bite from my breakfast. *Yes, I fucking did.*

"**U**ncle Ben, catch me." My daredevil nephew jumps off the climbing frame in my garden, full of trust that I will stop his fall. Luckily, I know him well and I'm always on high alert around him.

"Why don't we play a bit of football?" Coop asks, white as a sheet. I swear, if he ever becomes a father, Lizzie will have to keep a stash of chamomile tea or some other calming remedy handy. He's been a wreck dealing with all of Robbie's little stunts this afternoon

After he and Lizzie joined us for breakfast they stayed for lunch. My sister and Robbie came over as usual and I convinced Amelia to invite Miranda and Bri. I suggested Bea as well, but Amelia mumbled some excuse and just texted the two of them.

Five women in one house——Coop and I took Robbie outside to escape the laughter. Poor Smutty had enough of all the noise too and is probably hiding in one of the bedrooms.

"Football's boring," Robbie whines. Every time he tears apart my favourite sport, my heart bleeds for Aston Villa. It's like a dagger through my footballing soul.

"How about you carry on painting your bird house?" I ask him.

"Yes!" he cheers and sprints to the little shed at the end of the garden. We grab his equipment and the wonky bird house we nailed together——I'm shit at DIY, especially with the help of a pint-sized assistant like Robbie——but I tried my best. Once he's settled at the garden table he starts painting the roof a garish green. Not sure any birds will ever go into that monstrosity.

Coop stuffs his hands into his pockets. "So, how's it going with Amelia?"

"I told her I love her," I blurt out.

"And what did she say?"

"Nothing." I ruffle my hair.

"Does that worry you?" Coop's eyes are on me. *Does it?*

"I'm not sure. She seems to trust me so I don't think it's that. It feels like she loves me but she's just afraid to say it. Shi——" I catch myself. Fi doesn't like me swearing in front of Robbie. "Coop, I don't know. Maybe I'm just imagining it all or it is wishful thinking. But I'm willing to wait and find out." *Yes, yes, that's my plan.*

"And what if she never says it back?" *Fucking Coop and his pragmatism.*

"Then I'll wait for forever." I help Robbie squeeze more paint into the pot. Coop doesn't reply.

"Uncle Ben can I marry Amelia?" Robbie pipes up.

"Sorry?" I feel an actual twinge of jealousy, even if only for a few seconds.

"I like her."

"That's great, Robster but you don't need to marry her. You can just be friends."

"Oh, okay," he grins. *Crisis averted*. I already have to share her with Furball, I'm not sharing her with anyone else.

"You were jealous of a five-year-old there for a minute, weren't you?" Coop smirks.

"Don't be ridiculous," I huff but we both know he's right.

"Ben I don't think you'll have to wait long. Everyone can see that she loves you from the way she looks at you.

"You old sop," I chuckle, but his words make me grin. Let's hope he's right.

25

Moments We Live For

Amelia

SMUTTY WEAVES IN AND out between my feet as I stand at the window and stare down at the garden.

The girls are having a blast downstairs. Fi and Lizzie are getting on like a house on fire with Bri and Miranda and the noise level is accordingly high. No wonder the guys retreated outside.

I came upstairs to check on Smutty and found him curled up on Ben's pillow. After giving him some attention I was drawn to the window. For the last fifteen minutes

I've been watching Ben goof around with Robbie and their relationship makes me go weak in the knees. If Ben winking at me is catnip then Ben taking care of his nephew is a supersized bag of catnip.

Smutty bumps his head into my leg, a sure sign that he wants to be cuddled.

He curls up in my arms when I finally give him what he was begging for. His purring is calming and my mind drifts back to last night... and this morning. I can't remember ever experiencing sex like I'm having with Ben. Not even when we were younger. This is a new Ben.

He's attentive, he is caring, he's dominant, he is... hot and knows exactly what buttons to push, literally and figuratively speaking. I feel safe and I feel like me in his arms and these are two sensations I haven't felt in forever.

Movement in the garden catches my attention. Ben scoops up Robbie and makes him laugh out loud before they head to the shed and start taking out what appears to be art supplies.

I never thought of Ben as a father but there is no denying that he dotes on his nephew.

"Oh, Smutty, I think he's stealing my heart," I sigh. He rubs his little black head against my neck and chirps. "Yes, I know, he's already stolen yours."

"I CAN'T BELIEVE WE'RE doing this," I whisper as we walk into the shop with blocked windows.

"Oh, come on! You can date a pleasure dom but you can't go to a sex shop?" Samira rolls her eyes at me. I told her that I wanted to buy some nice underwear for Ben. I personally don't get the appeal because I don't tend to feel sexy in lingerie (more like a stuffed sausage), and I hate the feeling of the material on my skin. But if I play my cards right he'll just rip it off me and I won't have to wear it for long.

"Okay, what kinky stuff are you thinking about?" Samira grins.

"Nothing," I mumble and my cheeks pink up, of course.

"Stop blushing and let's see what we can get you." She struts towards the underwear section. There isn't much choice for underwear shopping near work and it was either this shop or Marks & Spencer, and Samira vetoed that because they only sell granny underwear. Her opinion, not mine.

"How about this?" she asks and holds up something that I'm not sure I know how to wear.

At my age my breasts no longer point upwards and instead droop downwards. They are soft and less firm, which means unless I have a full cup reining them in they'll find a way to mysteriously flow out of my bra in a very unsightly manner. It's like they turn to semi-fluid until they form some random bumps, making it appear like I have rippled breasts.

"Well, no!" I whisper-shout. Samira just shrugs and keeps browsing. I look around the underwear section until I spot a set that doesn't look quite that uncomfortable. I look for my size but they only have it a size smaller. But it's underwear. Sizing is not that accurate, right?

"I found some," I mumble.

"Well, try it on," Samira raises an eyebrow.

"No! I'll try it when I get home," I whisper. Ben has a business dinner so he'll be back home late. Plenty of time for me to give this a go before he gets home.

"Maybe I should get something for my husband." She lifts a tiny thong up. "I told him about Ben being a pleasure dom and he thinks I'm trying to trick him into 'servicing me'." She rolls her eyes dramatically. Samira has a lovely husband. She does complain about him regularly but deep inside she adores him.

"I had to Google the pleasure dom definition in the end to prove it to him."

"So, is he giving it a try?" I giggle as we stroll towards the cashier.

"No. Frankly, I don't think it's for me either. I'm not really the submissive type." She shrugs. "But we might try a swingers' club." I stop abruptly and she bumps into me.

"Samira!"

"What? Did Ben not tell you? As long as both parties consent and it's legal, it's okay. So, no sex-shaming here, Miss I'm-submitting-to-my-Ex," she winks.

Cue heat shooting back into my cheeks. I know, I know, I really need to get my shit together but I just can't help it. And Ben never makes me feel silly when I get embarrassed. I have a feeling he likes that side of me. I'll miss living at his when Smutty and I move back home on the weekend. My boiler is finally done and I should be elated but I'm not.

We grab a sandwich on the way back to the office and by the time we get there my tummy is rumbling.

"Amelia!" Graham calls out as I walk past his office. *Great, what now?* I hand my shopping bags to Samira and step into his office.

"Hi."

"The finance team has a complaint about this invoice. Anila emailed to say you refused to approve it. What is going on, Amelia?"

"Well, the invoice isn't mine so I can't approve it."

"It's for security analysis."

"I know."

"Amelia, who else would order an analysis?" He whines frustrated.

"Richard." I cross my arms in front of my chest.

"Are you assuming or do you know that?" he asks.

"I know." After I received the initial email from Anila I called the company and asked them who placed the order. I knew this would come back to me and I won't take it this time.

Graham types something on his computer and I see Richard rise from his desk. We are all obsessed with the internal messaging service and Graham clearly used it to summon the twat.

"What's up, Gra—" Richard grins at our boss, but ignores me.

"Did you order a security analysis for Balochistan?" Graham cuts off the little twerp, who is finally losing his smug expression.

"Yes, I needed it for—"

"Did you run it past Amelia?"

"No. You heard her, she—"

"Well, here's the invoice. It has to come out of your budget."

"What? But it's a security cost." He looks a bit panicked. I guess I'm not the only one with budget concerns.

"Yes, but I'd already told you that we won't approve a trip. I didn't authorise this expense and I don't have the budget. Next time, listen to me." My voice is strong and confident and I emphasise the word "listen". "Thanks, Graham," I say before leaving them both in the glass office. Amelia: One, Richard: Nil.

"So?" Samira asks when I get back to our desks, handing me my sandwich.

"Graham told Richard to pay the invoice from his budget." I can't help but feel smug. "I told Richard that next time he needs to listen to me." We both look towards Graham's fish-tank office and can see Richard getting a proper telling off from Graham.

This is probably my favourite day at work in a long time.

26

Nothing Is As It Seems

Ben

I CAN'T WAIT TO pick Amelia up and head home. It's been a long day of interviews for the new general manager and it showed me why we need someone in place sooner rather than later. I have no patience for long work days anymore.

Amelia moved back to her flat three weeks ago but we've still spent almost every night together. Furball has stayed as well because she can't leave him alone. I even got him a litter box and some toys so Amelia has less to carry back and forth.

Talking of Furball, he'll be waiting for us. I've got to confess, Smutty has wriggled his way into my heart, which Amelia loves to tease me about ever since she caught us last week. Furball's figured out that my body gives off the warmth he craves when he's asleep. He's got a thing for snuggling up inside my zip-up hoodie whenever I wear one. Do I find myself wearing them more often now because of him? Maybe, but I won't own up to that. Amelia returned from her spa day with the girls earlier than expected and caught me lounging on the sofa watching rugby with a big lump under my hoodie. And, of course, the moment she stepped in, the little rascal poked his head out of the top of the zip. It was like a feline reenactment of that scene in Alien.

There is no hiding it: I love him. Almost as much as I love her. I can feel a frown form on my face. I try to not let it bother me that when I tell her that I love her she doesn't say it back. I know she has issues and she needs to work her way through them in her own time. But I can't help the twinges of disappointment when the words don't come.

Omar indicates right and we pull up outside Amelia's workplace. Coop and I had a chat and decided we'll need to let Omar go once we hire a general manager. We're planning to cut back our hours significantly and it makes no sense to keep two drivers. We haven't told Omar yet and, I'm not keen to break the news. I'm still scrambling to work out how to keep him around until at least next year when he wraps up his degree. Chances are he'll be off doing bigger and better things by then anyway.

"She should be out soon," I tell him as I text Amelia that we are outside. I don't even get a chance to send the message before she pulls the door open.

"Hi Omar," she grins before placing a semi-passionate kiss on my lips. Not enough heat to embarrass Omar, but enough to tell me that she too can't wait to get home. *Sorry Furball, you're going to have a solo evening tonight.*

"Good day?" I ask her.

"Meh, work," she replies with a shrug. I suggested once that she could leave her job and I'd support her until she found something she enjoys. The explosion was epic and I won't open that can of worms ever again. Apparently, she can look out for herself.

She curls up in my arms and that tells me more than she could know. When she's needy for my touch she's had another frustrating day. Richard, the wanker, probably gave her shit again. Whenever that happens, she needs some silent time in my arms because I'm her safe place. I guess telling me this is almost the same as telling me she loves me. *Stop obsessing about that tiny detail.* I know my brain is right, but I can't help it. I'm dying to hear her say it because I know what a big deal it would be.

T HE FRONT DOOR FALLS heavily into the lock. I wink at Amelia as I drop my keys into the little bowl on the side table.

"Master kept his submissive waiting," a voice purrs behind me. Then, all falls quiet. Gina stands there in the doorway to the living room, clad in nothing but some lacy knickers and a bra. Amelia and I are caught off guard, frozen in place, our eyes locked on her. Gina gasps, eyes wide with shock.

"Gina?" I manage to shake off my stupor. *What is wrong with her?* I would have thought after the disaster with my sister she'd have learned to not rock up at my house half-naked.

"Oh, shit, Ben, sorry, I didn't know," Gina flinches as she nods at Amelia. "Hi, nice to meet you," she waves awkwardly and tries to slide her body out of sight.

"How did you get in here?"

"Your housekeeper remembered me," she says sheepishly. "Let me just grab some clothes." She holds up a finger to indicate one minute before returning to the living room.

"Amelia." I turn her and get her to look at me. "I don't know what she's doing here. I swear." I'm not sure why I immediately feel guilty because I've done nothing wrong but I'm painfully aware of what this looks like.

"Who is she?" Amelia whispers. She is pale and I definitely detect some sadness in her expression.

"Someone I dated casually in the past. We were more fuck buddies than actually dating, I haven't seen or been in touch with her in months," I try to explain with a neutral tone, desperate to hide any hint of panic. The last thing I want is for her to misinterpret it. The fear of losing her looms over me every single day, but it's never felt as intense as it does right now.

"He's right, I'm so sorry about this all. He didn't know I was planning to come over." Gina steps back into the corridor, now fully dressed. "Hi, I'm Gina." She holds out her hand to Amelia, who shakes it like it's the last thing in the world she wants to touch.

"Gina this is Amelia, my girlfriend," I introduce them. I gently rub Amelia's back to reassure her but she steps from my reach. *Shit!*

"Ben and I would... you know," Gina blushes, "whenever neither of us was in a relationship and Ben hasn't really been dating much. I broke up with someone a month ago and I thought I'll surprise him. I didn't know that he was seeing someone. I promise." She laughs nervously as Amelia stares at her. "Oh wait, is that THE Amelia," Gina lights up and when I nod, she adds to Amelia, "I've heard so much about you. Oh, my god, I'm so happy for you, Ben."

Amelia's stony expression tells Gina that she really doesn't have any interest in continuing the conversation.

"Well, I'll head out then. Again, I'm really sorry. Adorable cat," Gina rambles on before squeezing past us in the tight corridor and heading to the door.

"Amelia, I'm really, really sorry. I swear, I didn't know he's in a relationship and he had no idea I was planning to come," Gina whispers before giving us a last wave and leaving the house.

The minute we are alone I turn to Amelia. "Can we talk about this?" I start.

"There's nothing to talk about. You clearly didn't know. It's fine," Amelia brushes me off and heads towards the back of the cottage, calling out for Furball.

"Amelia—"

"It's fine," she interrupts me, but I can see on her face that it isn't fine. I don't think she disbelieves me but something has shifted and I feel a sense of doom. *Fuck!*

Smutty, as always oblivious to anything that doesn't concern him, rubs up to us as we make our way to the kitchen. He wolfs down his dinner and soaks up all the pats and scratches he can get. He absolutely enjoys being the buffer between us.

Amelia is trying to act normally but the darkness in her eyes tells me that her brain is working overtime. I've asked her if she's okay a few more times and all I've got was a short yes. I can't convince her that there's nothing to worry about if she shuts me out.

Now she is upstairs having a bath and I'm defrosting some beef stew even though I have no appetite. I wish she'd just tell me what's going on in her head so I could show her she has nothing to worry about. She is my life; she is my love.

The microwave beeps, and I jab the button with irritation as if it's the kitchen gadget's fault. When I yank the pot out, the makeshift cover I plonked on top decides to make a run for it. Steam billows into my hand, triggering a reflex that makes me jerk back. The pot escapes my grip, meets the floor with a resounding crash, and sprays beef stew all over the place——including my trousers.

"Fuck!" I shout. Furball jumps and is about to run from the kitchen when he spots one of the pieces of meat on the floor.

"Oh my god what happened?" Amelia asks from behind me. She manages to grab Smutty before he can sprint through the sauce in search for more meat and spread the disaster even further. She drops him into the corridor and closes the kitchen door on him. His little head pops up in the glass panel and he starts caterwauling.

"I dropped the food," I say like the bomb site needs an explanation.

"Wait, don't move," Amelia orders. There is beef sauce dripping from my trousers and I'm surrounded by a puddle of it. Amelia quietly starts mopping up our dinner and when she eventually gets to me she makes me take off my trousers.

"Did you burn yourself?" she asks as she gently touches my shins.

"No," I grumble. I can see red spots where the stew-soaked trousers have heated up my skin but it's not bad. Amelia takes my trousers to the utility room whilst I head upstairs to get clean clothes.

Smutty shoots pass me into the kitchen the minute I open the door and starts sniffing the floor, probably disappointed that he can't snag more premium beef.

When I get to the bedroom I take a deep breath. I need to get her to open up to me. My muscles are tense from anxiety. I decide to take a quick shower and after trying to relax under the hot water, I get dressed and head back down with a renewed determination to get her to talk to me.

I'm about to follow the noise of Amelia tinkering in the kitchen when my eyes fall on her suitcase. It's standing next to the door with the cat carrier.

"Amelia," I call out with my heart racing.

"Are you okay?" she asks with concern when she sees me. *No, I'm not okay.*

"Are you going somewhere?" My voice sounds harsher than I meant it to and I notice her flinch.

"Ben, I... we haven't been home in ages. I thought it would be a good time for me and Smutty to sleep at home tonight and check... the flat." She avoids my eyes.

"There is nothing between me and Gina. Yes, we dated in the past, but we haven't in a long time. I didn't know she was coming over." I cup her face and make her look at me.

"I know." She sounds small and sad when she replies. "I just——I just need to check on my flat."

"That's bullshit and you know it," I say, frustrated. She just shrugs. I wish she'd let me in. I feel so helpless. If she's not willing to talk about it there is nothing I can do.

"Oh my god we're just not staying here for one night. You won't die," she lashes out and I immediately see guilt on her face. "Sorry, I didn't mean to... Just give me a few days."

"Don't cut me out, Amelia. Please. Whatever is going on inside your head... or heart, I'll give you time, but please find the strength to talk to me about it. Please, don't throw this away over nothing," I beg and gently pull her into my arms. She lets me and that makes me breathe a little easier.

"I promise," she whispers against my chest.

"Okay." I let go of her even though every fibre in my body tells me not to. It takes us ten minutes to corner Furball who clearly has no desire to leave my house, but eventually we manage to wrangle him into his carrier.

"Don't forget your promise, Amelia," I whisper before kissing her deeply. The thought that this could be the last kiss we share almost kills me.

27

This Is What It Feels Like

Amelia

WHEN I STIR FROM my dream my chest feels tight and it's difficult to breathe.

When I made it home on Friday, Smutty punished me with an hour of crying and scraping on the front door, making it abundantly clear that he wanted to be with Ben. Once he had calmed down it took me ages to fall asleep.

Yesterday I spent all day in bed feeling sorry for myself.

My brain has been racing with random thoughts and questions. Was it all an illusion? I know they both said there's nothing between them and I believe them. But if that's the woman he dated before me, how can he now date me?

She was a fucking knock out. I mean, if I were into women I would date her. Just enough curves, covered by tiny pieces of underwear to look like every teenage boy's wet dream. With silky long hair, perfect facial features, big green eyes and pillowing lips. I can't compete with that.

I roll from bed and slide into my fluffy slippers. A quick look at my phone tells me it's already eleven o'clock and I'm surprised that Smutty hasn't come for cuddles yet. I find him on the window seat in the living room, lying on his belly and looking out the window completely ignoring me. Apparently he's still pissed with me.

His food bowl is empty but he doesn't react when I shake some dry food in it.

"Well fuck you then!" I shout and grab a banana, but I don't really feel like food either. I open the music app on my phone and press play on one of my playlists. I grab some rubber gloves and cleaning material. Isn't cleaning what they do in movies to help get over... heartbreak?

I start scraping the oven and frankly by the time I'm finished I feel neither better nor less sad. That's bullshit.

I fish my headphones from my handbag and place one in each ear. They automatically connect to my phone's

Bluetooth and the music which had been quietly playing in the background to avoid disturbing my neighbours is now blaring down my ear canals. It's so loud it actually drowns out my thoughts.

This is What It Feels Like comes on. I bloody love this song and it fits the mood perfectly. I start moving my body and dance to the living room. Smutty glares at me and jumps of the window seat, heading upstairs.

Whatever!

I close my eyes and sway from side to side. I'm not a fan of dancing in public unless it's mild shuffling like we did at the wedding. At home, though, I can go wild. Nobody cares if my movements are uncoordinated and completely out of rhythm.

I also don't sing generally. At most I'll lip-sync. I mouth the lyrics along as the artist sings about not knowing if he's alive. Yes, I definitely feel numb. Not quite unalive but not alive either.

I raise my arms and wave them to the beat of the music. This is the perfect pity party. I want to shake my head at myself. If I call him now, Ben will be here in an instant and I won't have to listen to a song about being alone. But instead, I start twirling and jumping, punching my arms in the air. My eyes are tightly shut.

The bass vibrates through me and I start to breathe a little heavier. Wild dancing is exhausting. I jump from one leg to the other as the music amps up the beat again and shout out the lyrics. *Fuck the neighbours.*

As the last notes echo out I open my eyes and drop on my sofa, breathing heavily. In the second of silence before the next song starts a soft knock to my right catches my attention.

Four figures are staring at me through the living room window. Big grins on their faces tell me that they've witnessed my concert performance. *Oh shit*, they probably even heard my out of tune singing. I pull my ear plugs out and switch off the music on my phone.

Miranda gestures towards the front door, and she, Fi, Lizzie, and Bri vanish from the window. For a brief moment I toy with the idea of hiding. *What a ridiculous thought!* Instead I heave myself off the sofa and sluggishly shuffle off, half-believing that approaching the door at a snail's pace might somehow boost the odds of them magically disappearing .

A harsh knock on the door tells me that I'm not in luck. *Fuck! Time to face the music.*

"Armin van Buuren, right?" Lizzie greets me and dances passed me, toeing her shoes off before placing them on the small shoe rack.

"What are you doing here?" I ask as Bri gently manoeuvres me aside so they can all crowd the entrance area, take off their shoes and jackets and make themselves at home.

"We have, pastries, chocolate, pizza, and ice cream. And Prosecco," Fi holds up a few shopping bags.

"I don't drink," I mumble.

"That's for me, babes," Bri grins.

"Ben called Coop," Lizzie explains and gives me a big grin. *Of course he did.*

"Okay... so what are you doing here?" I ask again.

"Well, Lizzie alerted us and we ambushed Ben earlier. Don't take this the wrong way, but he looks yummy half-asleep." Bri laughs. *Don't I know it.*

"He told us the whole story so we're here for an intervention," Miranda says, gently guiding me to the sofa.

"Let me get some glasses," I try to protest as she pushes me onto the sofa.

"On it," she replies and heads to my kitchen. She's been here often enough to find everything she needs.

"But before we stuff ourselves with a week's worth of calories tell us honestly, did he do anything wrong? Because if so we'll head back to his house and read him the riot act. When he told us the story it didn't sound like he did but, he's a guy; they never think they've done anything wrong," Lizzie babbles.

"He... he didn't do anything wrong," I say defiantly. *This is definitely my craziness.*

"Okay so what's going on then?" Bri asks.

"Wait for me, wait for me," Miranda shouts as she races back to the living room. The plates, glasses and cutlery on the tray rattling. The girls start dishing out the food and someone presses a plate with a slice of pizza in my hand.

"So?" Fi leans forward as if she can hear better that way. All eyes are on me.

"I met his ex...shag buddy. I guess. He says they never dated properly."

"Gina?" Lizzie asks.

"Yes." I confirm before taking a small bite of my pizza.

"Is there more?" Fi probes.

When I finish telling them what happened they all look more confused than before I started.

"I still don't get it," Bri says through a mouth full of crisps.

"She was stunning," I whisper. It already started to sound crazy in my own head; I can only imagine what it sounds like to them.

"Amelia, you're driving us crazy here. Can you say more than just one sentence at a time?" Miranda exhales in frustration.

"She. Was. Stunning. I can't compete with that. What she called a bra I could maybe cover one nipple with. And she was sweet and funny and seemed to be a nice person. He should be with someone like her."

They all stare at me and say nothing.

"Amelia," Fi sighs and pulls me into an embrace. "My brother loves you. I think he's always loved you which is why he never had any serious relationships after you ended it. He's sitting broken in his house because he's worried he's losing you again. You're who he wants."

"Now, maybe. But—"

"No, no. Tell me honestly, when you look into his eyes and he tells you he loves you what do you see?"

"He means it," I sniffle.

"You are his beaver," Fi says making Bri snort.

"I beg your pardon?" I can feel the first waves of laughter bubble up inside me.

"Beavers find each other and stay together forever," she explains.

"Oh, thank fuck that's what you meant because I love you all but I don't want to talk about your beavers," Bri laughs which makes me and Miranda burst out in giggles as well.

"Oh my god, no, no, that's not what I meant! Robbie made me watch a documentary about beavers yesterday and it was about how they mate for life," Fi explains with a red face.

"I know I sound crazy. He's been amazing ever since he came back into my life. But it's just, when I saw her, I just——if I were him, I would go for her."

"Let me ask you something. If one of the Hemsworth brothers knocked on your door and offered to shag you all over the house, would you drop Ben?" Miranda asks.

"No!" I protest.

"See," Bri grins.

"But Ben is hot. And funny, and smart and kind and ..."

"Great in bed?" Lizzie chuckles.

"No bedroom talk, that's my little brother," Fi protests.

"Why can't you believe he thinks the same about you?" Lizzie asks with a serious face.

"Because... because—"

"Amelia, when will you see yourself the way the world sees you? Do you look like a Victoria's Secret model? No, but who the fuck does? That man loves you, warts and all," Miranda gives me a tight hug. "I've known Ben for a long time now and I've never seen him so happy, content and relaxed as when he has you in his arms. Don't throw it away because of your insecurities."

I can't hold back my tears and I see Fi tear up as well.

"Let's make a deal," Lizzie suggests, "Whenever self-doubt kicks in you call us and we'll tell you how amazing you are."

"Thank you," I cry and I see Lizzie sniffle.

"Now we've sorted this problem and before you actually make me cry, ME, the ice queen as my ex so lovingly calls me, let's talk about something else. So what kinks is Ben into?" Bri grins making me and Miranda laugh through our tears and Fi protest again.

"How can I make it up to Ben?" I ask them.

"Babes, no need for that. He'll drop anything to be with you in a second," Miranda laughs. Maybe she's got a point but it doesn't cut it for me. He deserves an apology. He deserves to be shown that I understand he wants me. And he deserves me to show him how much I trust him. This whole thing was never about doubting him but about me not trusting that I'm good enough. Ben deserves a grand gesture.

28

Beautiful Things

Ben

THIS IS PROBABLY THE hundredth time I've checked my phone today. No message from Amelia.

Coop is right though. I need to fight for her.

The light at the entrance comes on as I push the key to the front door into the lock and turn it. The minute I open the door a black shadow races towards me making little purring noises.

"What are you doing here?" I bend over and scratch between his ears. Furball rubs up against me and makes meows. My heart starts beating faster. If the cat is here Amelia must be here.

"Amelia?" I call out. But there's no answer. I flick the light switch in the hallway and see her coat on the hook next to the door. She's definitely here. The kitchen and living room are dark.

"Amelia?" I call again as I take two stairs at a time to the first floor. "Amel—" I swallow hard when I take in the scene I find in my bedroom.

Amelia is lying on her side in sexy as fuck, purple underwear. Her blond locks are tied back by a purple scarf, spilling gracefully over her shoulders. Dozens of LED candles are spread throughout the bedroom dousing the room in flickering golden light. Images from the concert flash through my memory.

"Hi, Amelia," I say as I lean against the door frame, hands crossed in front of me.

"Sir," she says in a deep voice that isn't hers. I assume she's trying to sound sexy. I rub my hand over my mouth to try to hide my grin. *I love this woman.*

"What are you doing here?"

"I'm..." She reaches behind her and fiddles with her knickers in a less than sexy way. More like someone who is trying to pull their underpants from between their arse cheeks. "I'm here to seduce you. As an apology," she whispers and sits up.

"Apology?" I stay at the door mainly to keep distance between us because I want nothing more than to pull her in my arms, but this is her moment.

"Yes, Ben, I'm sorry." She climbs of the bed and crosses the distance between us barefoot. "I... I was an idiot. I... You said you loved me and I wanted to believe it, but I... And then Gina; and in my mind all my craziness took over and it was just a lot easier to count my losses than risk trusting you," she sniffles.

"Why didn't you talk to me?" I lean my forehead against hers and stroke her arms.

"Because I'm an idiot," she groans.

"Hey, don't talk about my girlfriend like that," I chuckle, placing a soft kiss on her lips.

"I'm still... you forgive me?" Her hands slide around my waist.

"There's nothing to forgive," I shake my head. And I mean it. She found her way back to me. That's all I care about. "What now?"

"Now I'm taking this shit off because it is the most uncomfortable underwear I've ever worn," she groans before unhooking her bra and pushing her knickers over her hips.

"I'm sorry, this was supposed to be sexy and sensual and all but I'm clearly not woman enough for that."

"I don't know about that. What I'm looking at is very sexy," I grin at her standing in front of me completely naked.

"Ben, I want you to tie me up." She blushes as she says the words and avoids my eyes. "And I want you to punish me." The mood in the room changes, becoming electric.

I gently lift her chin to make her look at me. "What?

"I was a bad girl, sir. Please, punish me." My heart races

.

"Do you consider tying up to be a punishment?"

"No, sir. That's for me." I love how her cheeks turn even pinker. Her eyes are wide and there is desire in them, but also the thing I have been craving so much. Complete trust.

"So you want me to punish you?" I smirk.

Amelia nods. "But no spanking," she whispers, dropping the submissive role for a second.

"I know darling." I kiss her on her forehead. "Lie down on the bed." *I know exactly how I'll punish her.*

Amelia climbs onto the mattress and lays down on her back. Her focus is on me. A glimmer of uncertainty dances across her features, adding a hint of mystery, yet her longing is unmistakable.

I undo the button on one of my cuffs.

"So, tell me, darling, why do you think you need punishment?" I roll the sleeve up to my elbow.

"I should have trusted you. I should have talked to you. I should have believed you," she sighs. "I'm sorry Ben!" She fiddles nervously with her fingers.

"Put your hands on either side of you and stop fidgeting," I command with a steady voice whilst I unbutton my other cuff. Rolling that sleeve up as well, I walk slowly to the bed and look down at her as she tries to be a good submissive. I'm not a poet but I wish I were so I could put how she makes me feel into words properly. I always knew I had lost a lot when she walked out of my life, but only now, that I have her back, I realise how much.

"Do you trust me?" My heart beats faster. Although I see the answer in her eyes I'm still nervous.

"Yes, I do, Ben. Sir." Hearing her say that is almost overwhelming.

The purple scarf wrapped around her hair feels silky soft as I pull it off.

"Hands above your head." I have barely finished the words when she does as I tell her. No hesitation. Just trust.

I gently tie one end of the scarf around her left wrist then weave the material through the slats of the headboard.

Once it's stretched enough I wrap the other end around her right wrist.

"How does that feel?"

"Okay," she nods enthusiastically.

"Good," I place another soft kiss on her forehead. She looks beautiful and I could look at her for hours. "So, you demand punishment. Let's see."

I kneel over her, one leg on either side of her hips. , I close my hand carefully around her throat and slide my thumb up towards her chin.

"Do you remember your wish to have someone tie you down and tell you all the things wrong with you?"

She nods, confusion and trepidation obvious in her expression. I bend forward and place my mouth next to her ear.

"Let's play a slightly different game," I whisper before gently biting her earlobe. A whimper tells me that she liked that.

"What kind of punishment would it be if I give you what you want? No, no." I sit back on my haunches and look down at her. "You're so beautiful, Amelia." I slide the fingers of my left hand slowly down her throat. "But you're so much more than just looks. When you're with me I feel happiness I've never felt before. I want to hold you. I want to listen to you tell me about your day. I want to kiss you. I want to just be with you until the end of time."

Her eyes widen. She realises what I'm planning to do.

"Ben, you don't have to—"

"Ah, ah, ah; who said you can talk? This is your punishment. No talking." I pull my tie from my neck, roll it up into a ball and hold it to her mouth which she willingly opens. We both know that if she wants to get rid of it she could just simply spit it out. But it's the gesture that counts. She's ready to give in to her submissive side.

"So where were we?" I stroke her bottom lip with my thumb. "Amelia, you think people don't like you or just tolerate you. Or just have you around because they want something from you but that's not true." She shakes her head in disagreement.

"If they cared so little for you, why was the first thing Fi and Coop said to me when I told them about our meeting that I must not hurt you again? Why, if you mean nothing to them, did the girls immediately demand to know what I'd done wrong when you walked away from me? Didn't they all ambush you earlier despite me telling them not to because they wanted to make sure you were okay?"

A single tear runs down her cheek and my instinct is to stop because I don't want to hurt her. But she needs to hear this.

"Coop told me I'd be a fucking idiot if I don't fight for you because you're the best thing that's ever happened to me. Robbie told me he wants to marry you." A muffled chuckle escapes her. "I don't want you in my life for any reason other than that I love you. You make me feel whole. When we broke up something was missing from my life, and nothing and no one could fill that gap." I cup her face. "If you knew what I feel when I look at you, you wouldn't doubt me anymore. There isn't much in life that scares me but the thought of losing you scares me more than dying. You are beautiful, funny, caring, smart, you bring joy to my life. I love your curves, I love your nerdiness, I even love your crazy cat. Most importantly: I. Love. You."

She blinks away another tear and I gently pull the tie from between her lips.

She opens her mouth but then stops herself.

"Good girl, you can speak," I whisper against her lips before kissing her.

"I love you too Ben," she says once I let go of her. Hearing the words I've waited so long for starts a fire in me. Our lips melt together in a passionate kiss before I remove myself.

"Now for the second part of your punishment," I say and wink at her before climbing off the bed. Crossing my arms I look down at her. She fidgets under my gaze but when I raise an eyebrow she stills.

"So beautiful," I repeat whilst my fingers draw a line between her breasts down to her bellybutton. Goosebumps spread on her skin. "Rule number one, your safe word is 'Brighton'. And don't worry: no spanking. What's your safe word?" I ask as I slowly unbutton my shirt. It's not that I'm planning to hurt her She's made it abandonly clear that she doesn't want spanking or any other form of painful punishment. But I want to give her that safety tool to reassure her. I won't do anything she doesn't want me to.

"Brighton," her voice sounds nervous.

"Rule number two, I say when you can come." She gasps.

"Sir I'm not sure if I can—"

"You will," I stop her arguing and stroke a finger over her pussy lips. She moans.

"What's rule number two?"

"I can only come when sir tells me to." There's desperation in her voice.

"Good girl," I praise and her eyes light up. My shirt lands on the floor as I unbuckle my belt. Amelia's eyes roam over my body until they find my dick. It's rock hard and tenting the soft material.

"This is what you do to me, Amelia." Her breath speeds up a little. This is as much torture for me as it is for her. Painfully slow, I draw my zip down and slide my trousers off. My boxers land on the heap of clothes on the floor and I take a few steps towards her with my stiff cock pointing upwards. I wrap my hand around it and Amelia's eyes watch closely as I give it a few lazy pumps.

"I can't wait to make love to you, Amelia." My hand squeezes my dick a little harder. "But not yet. I think you deserve to wait a little longer."

Another whimper tells me she's desperate. She'll enjoy this.

29

Love Me Like You Do

Amelia

T HERE IS TINGLING ALL over my body and It's difficult to control my breathing. I have never been so
desperate for him to touch me.

"Don't forget, only come when I give permission!"
Ben's eyes are dark and fiery.

I nod, unable to find my voice. Asking Ben to tie me
up like this is a big step. It means completely surrendering
to him. But the trust I feel for him now erases any and
all my fears. My heart thuds in my chest and my breath

comes a little faster. It's not fear, it's the anticipation of letting someone else take charge. The knowledge that he's in control just makes everything so much more intense.

He leans down and kisses me gently on the lips before standing up and walking over to the wardrobe.

"Where are you going?" I ask, trying to sound casual but failing miserably.

He turns and looks at me, his eyes twinkling with mischief. "I'm just going to get something from the drawer."

My heart skips a beat as I watch him reaching for something. My eyes don't leave him as he rummages around in the drawer for a moment before pulling out... a feather.

I let out a breath I didn't realise I was holding as he walks back over to me, trailing the feather lightly over my skin.

He kneels down next to me and smiles.

"Don't worry," he says softly. "I'm not going to hurt you."

"I know," I moan.

He leans down and kisses me again before trailing the feather slowly over my body, starting at my neck and working down to my toes.

It tickles like crazy and I squirm against the restraints, laughing.

"Someone's ticklish," he teases. "Should we do that again?"

I try to glare at him but it's hard when I'm giggling so much.

He continues to run the feather over my skin, focusing on my most ticklish spots. I giggle and try to get away from it, but there's nowhere to go. He has me completely at his mercy and he knows it.

The feather continues its torturous journey down my body until it finally reaches its destination——the space between my legs.

I gasp as he trails the feather lightly over my clit, sending tremors of pleasure coursing through me.

"Like that?" he asks with a smirk.

I can't even form words at this point so I just nod and bite my lip, trying not to moan too loudly.

He chuckles softly and puts the feather aside before leaning down and kissing me again. His lips are soft and gentle against mine as his tongue explores my mouth. I kiss him back eagerly, losing myself in the sensation of his lips on mine.

His hands roam over my body, touching me everywhere except where I want him most. It's frustrating as hell but incredibly arousing. By the time his fingers finally find their way between my legs I'm practically dripping with need.

He teases me for what feels like an eternity before sliding two fingers inside me. I moan into his mouth as he pumps them in and out, curling them slightly to hit that sweet spot deep inside me.

I'm so lost in pleasure that I almost don't notice when he adds a third finger. It stretches me deliciously as he fucks me with them, bringing me closer and closer to the edge with each thrust.

Just when I think I can't take it anymore Ben pulls away from me completely. I groan in frustration but am silenced by a stern look from him.

"Not yet," he says firmly. "You'll come on my cock."

"Yes sir," I reply obediently and a flash of lust passes over his face at my words.

I watch him intently as he grabs a condom before climbing back onto the bed. His cock is hard and throbbing, glistening with pre-come.

He rolls on the condom and positions himself between my legs. He takes hold of his cock, rubbing the head against my entrance teasingly. I moan loudly, desperate for him to fill me completely.

But instead of thrusting into me he moves his hand to the back of my knee and lifts my leg up, hooking it over his shoulder. He does the same with my other leg before he finally pushes into me.

I gasp as he stretches me open, filling me completely. He starts to move slowly at first, his hips rocking against mine in a gentle and languid rhythm.

Each thrust hits that spot deep inside me perfectly sending sparks of pleasure through my body. I'm already so close to the edge that it doesn't take long for pressure to start building again.

He picks up the pace gradually, each thrust harder and faster than the last. I cling onto the scarf desperately as he fucks me senseless.

My moans fill the room as I get closer and closer to my release. Ben's grip on my legs tightens as he pounds into me relentlessly.

Finally I can't hold back any longer.

"I need to come, sir." I fight the orgasm desperately. I don't want to let him down.

"Soon," he replies before moving faster.

Oh god, he's going to kill me if he doesn't let me come.

"Eyes on me, Amelia," Ben demands. I hadn't even realised that I'd closed them. "I'll count down from ten and then you can come. Do you think you can hold on that long?"

"Okay," I moan.

"Ten... nine... eight." I can see on his face that this is torture for him too. I suck the air deep into my lungs in the hope that this will stop the orgasm. "Seven... six... five... four."

Just before he gets to three, he moves one of his hands and starts circling my clit. I cry out, but just about can hold off my climax.

"Three... two... one... Come for me," he calls out.

The pressure inside me explodes like a supernova sending bolts of lightening through every nerve ending in my body.

I scream his name as the orgasm sets me alight, rendering me completely helpless and at his mercy.

Ben's movements become erratic as he chases his own release. He thrusts into me a few more times before stilling completely and groaning loudly.

We lie there for a few moments, our bodies still joined together. Eventually Ben leans down and kisses me softly on the lips before reaching for the scarf. He unties my wrists, takes of the condom and then slides his arms around me.

I snuggle against him happily, feeling safe in his embrace. We stay in silence for a while, lost in our own thoughts.

Finally I turn to look at him, a smile tugging at the corners of my lips. "That was amazing."

He grins at me and pulls me closer. "You were amazing," he corrects gently. "Thank you for trusting me."

I blush at his words. He knows what a big step for me this was and what this means for us.

He kisses the top of my head before resting his chin on it.

"I love you, Amelia," he says quietly.

"You are the love of my life, Ben. Thank you for never giving up on me."

30

Perfect

Epilogue

Ben

O<small>H, THAT IS DISGUSTING.</small>

"Furball!" I shout as I toe off my football boots. A grey slimy mass is stuck to the bottom of my sock. Lately Smutty's favourite place to vomit is my shoes.

A tiny black head peeks around the corner. He knows what he's done and he will avoid me and repay me with extra snuggles this evening. I know his routine by now. I take my sock off carefully to avoid dropping any of the slime on the floor and take it to the laundry room together with my soiled boots.

Me

> Furball left me a present in my boots.
> I'll have to wash them so unless one
> of you has a spare pair for me I'll have
> to give football a miss today.

Coop and I have joined my brother-in-law in the village football team. Robbie was annoyed because it meant we had to move our weekly lunch, but now that I have more time I usually take Fridays off and we meet then.

Hiring a general manager was the best idea Coop ever had. She's amazing and we both feel that soon we'll only have to go into the office a couple of times a week. The only thing that would complete our happiness is if Amelia and Lizzie had a bit more free time. But these are two stubborn women.

Coop

> Don't worry! We just got here and the
> rain from yesterday has turned the
> pitch into a lake. I'm heading home
> to Lizzie.

Me

> Great!

"You are one lucky cat," I tell Furball, who's sitting at a safe distance in the kitchen watching me scrape his vomit from my boot. When he hears the front door Smutty shoots into the corridor probably with the aim of begging for some belly rubs.

"Hey Mister, see this? Now you won't be able to vomit in Ben's shoes anymore," Amelia giggles.

"Too late darling," I hold up exhibit A.

"Ben, what are you——" Her eyes drift to Smutty. "Not again. I'm so sorry. But I bought you a shoe rack with doors so he can't get to your shoes anymore." She points at the box next to her.

"You bought us a shoe rack," I correct her before dropping my boot on the floor.

"I don't live here," she protests but willingly snuggles up in my arms when I hold them out to her.

"You would if I had my way." I mean, she basically is. She stays here every night. Every so often she makes a weak attempt at suggesting to sleep at her flat but me and Furball gang up on her. He hides from her and I refuse to help her look for him. In the end, we win and everyone is happy.

"Ben!"

"Let's be practical here; you pay a lot of rent each month and for what?"

"Well, maybe Smutty and I should sleep at home more often," she suggests and places a soft kiss on my chin.

"Wrong! Give up your flat."

"And then what?"

"Move in here," I grin.

"What's the rent?" *Shit, this is different, is she going to give in?* She better not be toying with me.

"No rent."

"I have to pay rent," she protests.

"Why?"

"Because——"

"Excellent argument," I chuckle. ", This house is paid off. I don't pay rent. This house is mine, there's no mortgage on it, nothing. Come on. Just move in."

I see the conflict in her eyes.

"Please," I beg. Yes, I'm not ashamed to do that. "I can guarantee you daily orgasms," I whisper.

"Ben!" she laughs but then relaxes in my arms. "Fine, I'll call my landlady on Monday."

"You're making me very happy."

"Yeah, yeah, you just want someone to bake you cakes," she jokes but there's joy in her face.

I pick up my boot from the floor and head back to the utility room.

"How was therapy?" I call out. Amelia is emptying groceries from her shopping bag into the fridge.

"Good, she encouraged me to talk with you about something I've been meaning to bring up," she says casually, but her body is tense.

"What is it?" I drop on one of the stools next to the breakfast bar.

"I... I was wondering how you would feel about a trip up north."

"Sure. Any time. Why were you worried to ask?" I'm confused.

"It would be for three months." She nervously nibbles her bottom lip.

"Three months? What are you planning to do, climb every Munro in the Lake District?" I laugh.

"No, there's this art course in Yorkshire. And it looks amazing. You have lessons twice a week and you can practice different crafts." Her eyes light up. Her therapist has encouraged her to find a new hobby as she didn't really have anything aside from travelling and Smutty. She tried yoga and had an unfortunate farting incident and now she refuses to go back. She joined a cooking class and burned her first dish. She took up baking but there's only so much cake we can eat. And then she discovered working with clay and loves it.

I turned one of the guest bedrooms into a small art studio for her and when I say "I", I mean I paid proper professionals to do the work. She protested at first but gave in and I had another reason to keep her here.

Every Sunday Robbie comes over to have a craft session with her. She's even helped him build a proper bird house. Amelia found her thing, and I'll support her where I can.

"Sounds good to me," I smile.

"Are you sure? It might be quite boring for you. But I found this farmhouse with a hot tub and we can bring Smutty and maybe Coop and Lizzie can visit, and——"

"Amelia," I stop her, "I don't need to be entertained. I can use the time to maybe find my own hobby. I quite like to try my hand at writing or something."

"Oh?"

I shrug. "Why not?"

"And what would you want to write?" She nibbles my earlobe. I love when she does that.

"Hm, a publisher I know is pushing me to write about business. So maybe on how being a pleasure dom helps with business."

"Ha, what like *Boss in the Bedroom, CEO in the Boardroom*," she giggles.

"*Whip Your Career Into Shape: Pleasure Dom Style*," I say with a groan because Amelia is still attacking my ears, in a good way.

"Uh." She moves away and looks at me. "I love that. That title is amazing. You should so do that."

"Hang on, I was joking." But the idea sounds quite good to me too.

"Write it down."

"What?"

"Write it down Ben, before you forget." I sigh and grab my phone. I send myself an email with the subject line *Possible Book Title*.

"Happy?"

Amelia nods. "So does this mean we can go to Yorkshire for three months? I mean I also have to check with work but—"

"Of course we can, and fuck work. If they don't give you the time off you quit and look for something else afterwards. I'm here for you and I would go anywhere with you. As long as you're with me——"

"And Smutty," she interjects.

"And Furball," I agree. "I love you Amelia, and I don't care if I do that here, in Yorkshire, or at the end of the world."

"Sir, please take me to bed and show me how much you love me," she moans seductively.

I'm the luckiest arsehole on the planet.

Thank you for taking the time to read
The Unnatural Habitat of a Cat Lady
Please spare a minute to leave a review on Amazon, Kobo
and Goodreads! Even a short sentence or two helps.

Want More?

Find out how Coop convinced Lizzie that he is "The One" in
Valentine's Rebellion

Join Bri and Omar on roadtrip full of surprises
The Unconventional Journey of a Cat Lady

Chapter / Playlist

CPT	TITLE	ARTIST
1	FUCK YOU	LILY ALLEN
2	PLAY WITH FIRE	SAM TINNESZ
3	IF I COULD TURN BACK TIME	CHER
4	ALL OR NOTHING	CHER
5	BELIEVER	IMAGINE DRAGONS
6	GIMME! GIMME ! GIMME !	ABBA
7	CRASH! BOOM! BANG!	ROXETTE
8	YOU ARE THE REASON	CALUM SCOTT
9	HUNGRY EYES	ERIC CARMEN
10	CURIOSITY	BRYCE SAVAGE
11	TRY LOSING ONE	TYLER BRADEN
12	BLEEDING LOVE	LEONA LEWIS
13	LIKE A VIRGIN	MADONNA
14	HOLDING OUR FOR A HERO	BONNIE TYLER
15	SMELLY CAT	PHOEBE BUFFAY
16	GREAT BALLS OF FIRE	JERRY LEE LEWIS
17	IF YOU DON' T LOVE YOURSELF	THE SCRIPT
18	TIME AFTER TIME	CYNDI LAUPER
19	BREATHE	MIDGE URE
20	MAMMA MIA	MARYL STREEP

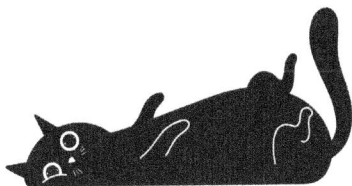

Chapter / Playlist

CPT	TITLE	ARTIST
21	SERENADE NO.13	W. A. MOZART
22	FROM NOW ON	HUGH JACKMAN
23	MAN ON A MISSION	OH THE LARCENY
24	ALL OF ME	JOHN LEGEND
25	MOMENTS WE LIVE FOR	IN PARADISE
26	NOTHING IS AS IT SEEMS	HIDDEN CITIZENS
27	THIS IS WHAT IT FEELS LIKE	ARMIN V. BUUREN
28	BEAUTIFUL THINGS	BENSON BOONE
29	LOVE ME LIKE YOU DO	ELLIE GOULDING

Listen Now:

https://bit.ly/3TwlQvS

Stay in Touch

Never miss a new release: Sign up for my newsletter to be the first to hear about free content, new releases, cover reveals, sales, and more: www.daniebooks.com/sign-up

You can also join the new reader Facebook group where you can meet other like-minded readers, pick up some exclusive giveaways and stay up-to-date with everything that is happening in my book world. I will have three big announcements in the next couple of months and you don't want to miss them!

You can join the Facebook group here:

https://bit.ly/3Cn5PQJ

More from Dani Elias

Fellside Mountain Rescue Series

Do you want to meet the guys from the Fellside Mountain Rescue Team?

Blossom with Me

Sing with Me

Paint with Me

Climb with Me

Read with Me

Build with Me

Wrap Up with Me

Ride with Me

Or binge the whole series:

Love at Fellside Vol. 1& Love at Fellside Vol. 2

Cat Ladies Rule The World

You know those "Cat Lady" myths? Forget 'em! These women are way more than meets the eye. They're not just crazy for cats – there's a whole lot more brewing beneath the surface. Picture this: romance, comedy, and a hint of kink. These books? They're like a rollercoaster ride through the love lives of forty-something ladies who redefine what it means to be a cat lover.

Valentine's Rebellion (Prequel Novella)

The Unnatural Habitat of a Cat Lady

The Unconventional Journey of a Cat Lady

Greenview Manor Tales

Get ready to meet the staff and guests of the **Greenview Manor Hotel**. Explore lost loves, new passions, and hidden romances in these five novellas, brimming with intense emotions and enough suspense to keep you on the edge of your seat.

Fierce Family
Alluring Adventure
Elusive Embrace
Wistful Whispers
Spellbinding Spirit

Aftermath

When aid workers Will, Melanie, and Jon find themselves tangled in an incident with devastating consequences, throwing them into a world of chaos and despair. Can their loved ones help them find their way back to life?

Mission

Escape

Rescue

Printed in Great Britain
by Amazon